MISSION ACCOMPLISHED:

A Practical Guide to Risk Management for Nonprofits

2nd Edition

by Peggy M. Jackson, Leslie T. White,
and Melanie L. Herman

**Nonprofit
Risk Management
Center**

ACKNOWLEDGEMENTS

The Nonprofit Risk Management Center is grateful to the following persons who served as reviewers for this publication:

Ilish Donnelly
American Specialty Risk
    Management Services
Washington, DC

David L. Mair
Associate Director for Risk Management
United States Olympic Committee
Colorado Springs, CO

H. Felix Kloman
Editor, *Risk Management Reports*
Lyme, CT

Linda P. Varnado
American Red Cross
San Antonio, TX

NONPROFIT RISK MANAGEMENT CENTER

The Nonprofit Risk Management Center is dedicated to helping community-serving nonprofits control risk so they can achieve their missions. The Center provides a range of services, including publications, training, and technical assistance. The Center is an independent organization operating under Section 501(c)(3) of the Internal Revenue Code. The Center's operations are supported by generous grants from public foundations and the Corporation for National Service, income from the sale of publications and delivery of training and consulting services, and corporate donations.

Staff
Greg Geddes, *Publications Manager*
Suzanne Hensell, *Director of Marketing and Education*
Melanie L. Herman, *Executive Director*
Dennis M. Kirschbaum, *Manager of Information Technology*
John Patterson, *Senior Program Director*
Leslie T. White, *Director of Risk Management Services*

CORPORATION FOR NATIONAL SERVICE

The Corporation for National Service engages Americans of all ages and backgrounds in community-based service. This service addresses the nation's education, human, public safety, and environmental needs to achieve direct and demonstrable results. In doing so, the Corporation fosters civic responsibility, strengthens the cords that bind us together as a people, and provides educational opportunities for those who make a substantial commitment to service.

ISBN 1-893210-01-4

Table of Contents

Preface

The year was 1859. A coach carrying Swiss businessmen rumbled through the Italian countryside. When the coach reached a meadow outside the tiny village of Solferino, Henri Dunant, the group's leader, signaled the driver to stop. The French army had just dealt the retreating Austrians a decisive defeat in Solferino, and the meadow was littered with the bodies of four thousand dead and wounded soldiers. Dunant and his colleagues spent the next eight days tending the sick and wounded. That experience inspired Dunant to form the International Red Cross, an organization whose mission continues to this day — to mitigate the suffering of war. For the tireless work that began with a single selfless act, Dunant received the first Nobel Peace Prize.

Would a modern-day Dunant feel free to act so impulsively on his desire to ease the suffering of others? Or would he also have to consider the potential for liability inherent in his good deeds? Every year, many nonprofits are formed on good intentions. Those that succeed generally recognize not only the importance of their mission, but also the dangers of doing good in the twenty-first century.

Of course, few nonprofit managers will ever find themselves in the kind of dramatic scenario that altered Dunant's life. The real-life battles faced by nonprofit managers today center on such issues as funding, staffing, and managing service delivery in an increasingly litigious world. Implementing a comprehensive risk management program can avert missteps and mishaps and reduce threats to an agency's mission.

Risk management provides an invaluable set of tools for use by conscientious nonprofit CEOs, managers, and volunteer leaders. Risk management planning starts with an examination of core operations and the categories of assets the organization can't afford to squander — including people, property, income, and goodwill. Throughout the process, you determine the levels of risk your organization can withstand and the cost-effectiveness of activities you could take to minimize risk. This examination extends to service delivery programs, fund raising activities, administrative operations, and governance. A comprehensive approach to risk management allows you to make the right choices and take control over the areas that are most likely to cause financial loss or to damage your organization's reputation.

This guide offers a theoretical framework for risk management planning and practical strategies for putting risk management practices to work in a nonprofit setting. Our suggestions are offered with the overall goal of helping nonprofits achieve their community-serving missions.

As presented in this guide, risk management need not be a costly or protracted endeavor. Instead, practicing risk management is an essential step in conserving resources, protecting people from harm, and freeing up resources that should be dedicated to mission-related functions.

The Guide begins in *Chapter One* by presenting a framework for understanding the concepts behind the general topic of risk management and leads the reader through the steps of developing a risk management program. We keep the number of steps down to the minimum — we promise!

■ *Chapter Two* states in greater detail the case for developing a risk management program and explains risk management as it applies to four categories of assets at risk: people, property, income, and goodwill. The chapter illustrates some common scenarios which might expose an organization to liability, and the effect that these troublesome situations can have on the assets of most nonprofits.

■ *Chapter Three* describes the risk management process and the four steps in the development of a risk management program. The chapter also explains how to evaluate and use tools and techniques appropriate for controlling specific risks and discusses insurance as one option for financing risk.

■ *Chapter Four* features a discussion of special risks facing community-serving nonprofits. Selected topics include information-age risks; volunteer recruitment, supervision and liability; special events liability; crisis management; employment practices liability; transportation risks; serving vulnerable populations; collaboration risks; and grants management.

■ *Chapter Five* is a risk management glossary offering easy-to-understand definitions of risk management, liability, and insurance terms.

■ *Chapter Six* lists risk management resources and includes an annotated bibliography of risk management literature and resource organizations.

We hope that *Mission Accomplished: A Practical Guide* serves two purposes for every reader. First, the text is offered to support and guide an overall effort to examine and manage the risks that threaten your organization. The text explains risk management and its importance and relevance to your organization. After reading the book, you will be on your way to developing a comprehensive risk management program for your organization. Your first mission is accomplished.

The dangers facing your organization are real and if uncontrolled could prevent your nonprofit from achieving its mission. An unexpected loss or damage to an organization's reputation can prevent a nonprofit from providing the services vital to its constituencies. Our second purpose is to illustrate how your clients, employees, volunteers and the organization itself can be protected against harm through careful planning and a sincere commitment to safety. By incorporating risk management into your nonprofit's operations and culture, you will ensure that scarce resources are used most productively. In this manner, a risk management program is important if not invaluable to preserving and fulfilling the core mission of your nonprofit.

CHAPTER 1

What is Risk?

In the context of nonprofit risk management, *risk* can be defined simply as *any uncertainty about a future event that threatens your organization's ability to accomplish its mission*. The word "risk" derives from the Italian word *risicare*, which means "to dare." For our purposes, the roots of the word seem particularly apt. According to author and educator Peter Bernstein, "risk is a choice rather than a fate." The more you learn about the possibilities of risk management, the more applicable this statement seems for community-serving organizations.

WHO MANAGES RISK?

Risk management is *a discipline for dealing with the possibility that a future event will cause harm*. Because it is a way to anticipate and manage future events, risk management incorporates a decision-making process to determine how best to deal with the *potential* for loss. In the nonprofit sector, risk management focuses on identifying and dealing with risk as it applies to an organization's people, property, income, and goodwill.

Identifying risk in terms of cost and timing is important. While many risk management decisions take place in anticipation of loss, a solid risk management decision-making process is also essential in the wake of a crisis for damage control. Therefore, effective risk management assists the organization not only in helping to prevent loss — but also in coping with a loss once it has occurred.

Risk management is a pragmatic process with real-world implications. An organization cannot simply craft a plan and then put it on the shelf. Risk management is a way of thinking that must permeate the whole organization — from the most senior board member to the CEO to the newest volunteer. Understanding that dealing with risk is everyone's responsibility ensures that risk management becomes an integral part of the organization's life.

WHAT ARE THE GOALS OF RISK MANAGEMENT?

Risk management seeks to ensure the organization's continued ability to perform its mission, grow and maintain good health, and preserve its social responsibility to the community at large. Because every nonprofit has a responsibility to the public as well as to its clients, maintaining the public trust is essential for the organization's continued existence.

The more effective the risk management program, the more confident the board, executives, staff, and volunteers can be that their organization's mission and operations will be achieved. This guide will illustrate strategies for incorporating risk management and will demonstrate that risk management need not be expensive, time-consuming, or labor intensive.

CAN'T RISK BE ELIMINATED?

Risk is an inherent part of existence; an active community-serving organization cannot eliminate all threats. On the contrary, community-serving nonprofits generally must accept some risk in order to accomplish their missions. Therefore, a risk management program does not seek to eliminate all risk within an organization. Instead, it provides a framework for balancing and understanding which risks are inherent within the organization and for empowering staff to make good choices in dealing with these risks.

Even if a nonprofit organization develops and implements an outstanding risk management program, the organization still faces the possibility that a client may be injured or the organization might be sued — even for frivolous reasons. Responding to the legal summons in a lawsuit is compulsory, and defending the organization requires the expenditure of funds and the use of human resources. An effective risk management program can simplify the process by enabling the nonprofit to demonstrate that it followed the

appropriate steps or procedures in its activities — evidence that could help the organization prevail in a lawsuit.

DOESN'T INSURANCE COVER THE RISKS FACED BY AN ORGANIZATION?

Often nonprofit managers believe that simply purchasing insurance eliminates risk. As we will see in *Chapter Three*, insurance is a means of transferring your financial risk to another party. Simply purchasing insurance does not reduce the likelihood of a mishap, nor does it eliminate many aspects of non-financial risk to a nonprofit.

Although the third party, usually an insurance company, agrees to assume a degree of financial obligation for losses, the nonprofit continues to have responsibility for managing the risk. In addition, losses can lead to increases in insurance premiums, and in some cases, the cancellation of a policy. Securing similar coverage through another carrier could be problematic, or very costly.

Illustration 1

WHEN DOES THE RISK MANAGEMENT PROCESS END?

Illustration 1 depicts risk management as a circular process. Each of the four steps of the risk management process —

(1) identify risk, (2) evaluate and prioritize risk, (3) implement selected risk management techniques, and (4) monitor and update the risk management program — is connected to the steps that precede and follow it.

As the organization identifies risks, and crafts and implements risk management techniques, the process continues by requiring ongoing scrutiny of strategies and exposures. Because all organizations change over time, risk management processes, approaches and techniques must adapt to organizational changes. Risk identification, evaluation/prioritization, and the implementation of risk management activities support each other and are, in turn, dependent upon the orderly management and control of risk.

The process is a continuous loop. Risk management is not a one-time activity. As the nonprofit takes each step in the risk management process, it logically leads to the next until, eventually, this process is fully integrated into the life of the organization. In order to be successful, risk management must also be a consciousness-raising activity. Everyone — board members, executives, staff, and even volunteers — must understand what risk management is about and what role each person within the organization plays in promoting safety, minimizing the likelihood of accidents, and responding appropriately when precautions fail and an accident occurs.

WHY DOES EVERY NONPROFIT ORGANIZATION NEED A RISK MANAGEMENT PROGRAM?

Risk management programs should motivate everyone in the organization to consider the consequences of their actions. Nonprofit organizations need risk management programs because:

1. RISK MANAGEMENT CAN HELP AN AGENCY PROTECT CLIENTS, VOLUNTEERS, STAFF, AND THE GENERAL PUBLIC FROM HARM.

Because the focus of many nonprofits is to serve the community, the idea that any of its activities might harm or do disservice can be difficult for the board and staff of a nonprofit to comprehend initially. However, it is only when a nonprofit organization begins to understand what can go wrong that it can identify the strategies needed to prevent accidents, avoid procedural mistakes, and minimize the potential for errors in judgment that can rob the organization of the credibility and public trust it needs to remain viable.

Risk management is a means for a nonprofit to examine the safety of its physical plant, the fairness of its criteria for service delivery, the methods by which it serves clients, the manner in which it trains volunteers, and the quality of the organization's interactions with the public. Risk management also provides methods for examining board affairs, including the degree to which the board fulfills its governance and legal responsibilities.

2. THE NUMBER OF CLAIMS AND LAWSUITS FILED AGAINST NONPROFIT ORGANIZATIONS CONTINUES TO RISE.

Defending a nonprofit in a lawsuit costs money. Either the organization's insurer or, if there is no insurance, the organization itself pays the cost of legal defense. An effective risk management program strengthens the possibility that the nonprofit can prevail in litigation. In the past, charitable organizations were protected from litigation by virtue of their charitable status. This legal defense was known as charitable immunity. However, the tradition of protection from litigation because of charitable status has suffered in recent years through numerous reversals in the courts. Nonprofit organizations can be sued successfully and judgments collected. Although lawsuits are rare, the courts expect nonprofit managers and boards to know about and comply with legal rules and to exercise prudent judgment in managing the organization's affairs.

A nonprofit can be held liable for its own actions (direct liability) as well as the actions of persons acting on its behalf (vicarious or imputed liability). Vicarious liability is justified on the grounds that the entity that *directs* and *benefits from* an individual's actions should bear the costs of any resulting harm. Vicarious liability is often described using the antiquated terms "master" and "servant." The Latin phrase *respondeat superior* ("let the master answer") refers to the concept that a master is liable in certain cases for the negligent or wrongful acts of his servant. A "servant" is an individual who performs services for the benefit of and at the direction of another person or legal entity, the "master." The imposition of vicarious liability does not depend on a finding that the "master" was negligent or at fault in any way. The only questions are whether a "master-servant" relationship existed and whether the servant's negligence caused the harm. The courts have reasoned that since nonprofits have some measure of control over the activities of their paid and volunteer staff, they are in position to take precautions against injuries caused by them.

Why would anyone sue a nonprofit? Some of the reasons include:

- Violation of the state's charitable solicitation act.
- Wrongful termination.
- Defamation of character or invasion of privacy for inappropriate release

of confidential information on a client or volunteer.

- Bodily injury.
- Employment discrimination.
- Breach of contract.

Some lawsuits result from decisions made by the nonprofit's management or board. The nullification of the doctrine of charitable immunity forces nonprofit organizations to review their responsibility for the consequences of the actions of management, paid staff, and volunteer staff.

To avoid discouraging the impulse to volunteer, state legislatures have enacted legislation that provides varying levels of immunity for certain categories of volunteers. In addition, the Volunteer Protection Act of 1997 (VPA), signed by the President in June 1997, provides limited immunity for volunteers. However, the immunity provided by various state laws and the VPA is very narrow. As a result, community-serving nonprofits and their volunteers are exposed to potential liability in a host of areas. Even in those instances where a nonprofit is likely to prevail, the time and money required to defend an action may be considerable.

3. ACCIDENTS, CRISES, AND ADVERSE SITUATIONS ARE OFTEN PREVENTABLE.

A case in point: Mary spent six weeks on disability because of a painful knee injury sustained on the job when she slipped on water someone in the office had spilled on the coffee room floor and neglected to wipe up with a paper towel. Ten seconds of care could have eliminated six painful and expensive weeks — not counting the weeks of physical therapy to come — for Mary and her employer. Clearly, this injury was preventable.

Implementing a risk management program can minimize workplace risks by identifying potentially hazardous conditions that might contribute to a future loss. In addition to workplace risks, other areas of operations that pose potential hazards and require risk management attention include hiring practices, production activities, fund-raising activities, and work with high-risk clientele, such as individuals undergoing treatment for substance abuse.

The conduct of the board, staff, and volunteers, particularly in a time of crisis, is another area of potential risk. Community-serving nonprofits can utilize risk management techniques in developing procedures to manage and prepare for situations before they occur. It is particularly important to understand that the public sees board, staff, and volunteers as representatives of the community-serving nonprofit. By articulating clear expectations for their conduct, a nonprofit can prevent potential losses arising from the conduct of its people.

Because risk management activities have the potential for identifying areas within the organization that pose potential threats, the process of risk management offers a means for minimizing the possible damage.

4. AN EFFECTIVE RISK MANAGEMENT PROGRAM IS CRITICAL WHEN ENTERING INTO JOINT VENTURES WITH PUBLIC SECTOR AGENCIES OR CORPORATIONS.

Governmental entities generally require community-serving nonprofits engaged in joint ventures to present evidence of appropriate insurance coverage or fiscal responsibility. If a governmental entity requires insurance or another source of financial recovery as a condition of the venture, the nonprofit will have to provide either evidence of insurance or other financial resources. The

organization's process of obtaining sufficient insurance coverage at a reasonable price may be easier with an effective risk management program in place.

In addition, joint ventures or collaborative efforts are themselves inherently risky. A risk management program will assist the board and executive director in identifying areas of the agreement that pose risk for their organization, developing strategies to deal with the sometimes unique risks of such ventures, and determining whether the benefits of the venture outweigh the risks.

5. A RISK MANAGEMENT PROGRAM CAN IDENTIFY CIRCUMSTANCES THAT COULD CONTRIBUTE TO A CRISIS IN PUBLIC CONFIDENCE OR RESULT IN NEGATIVE PUBLICITY.

Few nonprofit boards or executives stop to consider the long-term effects of negative publicity on the organization's ability to raise funds, enter into joint ventures with governmental agencies, or even to remain in operation. Because nonprofit organizations have constant interaction with the public, the public and media often scrutinize almost every facet of a nonprofit's existence. Risk management activities work to identify hazards that would diminish the public's confidence in the organization or generate negative publicity.

For example, as nonprofit organizations grow in size and programmatic stature, their internal controls do not always keep up with the growth — with potentially disastrous results. *A case in point:* One prominent AIDS service provider grew so rapidly that it suddenly found itself with five separate "headquarters" within a large city. It entered into a government-funded housing program without first establishing the internal financial controls necessary to manage the program. Soon, allegations of misappropriated funds began to emerge and a scandal broke. As a result, the agency lost the government contract, and most of its donor base. Further, the local government's AIDS office forced the agency to join a collaborative arrangement that mandated oversight by another service provider.

Eight years later, the agency still exists, but as a shadow of its former self. It is still trying to win back the public confidence and private donors it squandered. The real tragedy is that this crisis need never have occurred! If the agency's board and executive management had recognized the inherent danger in a decentralized structure and lack of internal controls, they could have taken steps to avoid this crisis.

6 *A RISK MANAGEMENT PROGRAM HAS THE POTENTIAL TO MAKE THE ORGANIZATION ATTRACTIVE TO COMPETENT BOARD MEMBERS.* The board of directors is the primary center of power and responsibility within a nonprofit organization. Unlike private sector organizations, nonprofits do not have shareholders or grant seats on the board to individuals who own large portions of corporate stock. Competition for community leaders who would be productive board members is very keen. Individuals who have the potential to be excellent board members are often aware of the role that board decisions could play in incurring liability for the organization — and for board members individually.

The implementation of a risk management program can illustrate to potential board members that the organization takes its responsibilities to its clients and the community seriously. The presence of a risk management program demonstrates to potential board members, and to the community at large, the organization's commit-ment to maintaining its health and viability.

7. *A RISK MANAGEMENT PROGRAM HELPS PROTECT THE VIABILITY OF A NONPROFIT AND PRESERVE DONOR AND PUBLIC TRUST.* Why should nonprofit executives and boards care about public trust? Nonprofit boards have legal duties mandated by state law and responsibilities documented by the organization's articles of incorporation or bylaws. The responsibilities of the organization extend to the actions of the board and the entire staff, paid or volunteer. These factors heighten the role that risk management plays in the nonprofit sector because nonprofit programs contribute not only to the well-being of the organization's clients, but also to the community at large.

Community associations, the predecessor to modern-day community-serving nonprofits, have been part of American society since the first settlers arrived in the early seventeenth century. In his book, *America's Nonprofit Sector: A Primer*, Lester Salamon, Director of the Johns Hopkins Institute for Policy Studies writes, "Society predated the state . . . communities were formed before government structures . . . people had to tackle problems on their own." Alexis de Tocqueville, the great chronicler of American life in the 19th century, observed that community associations in America were formed for an array of reasons. "Americans of all ages, all stations in life . . . are forever forming associations. There are not only commercial and industrial associations . . . but others of a thousand different types — religious, moral, serious, futile, very general . . . and very minute [small]."

Community-serving nonprofits offer individual citizens the opportunity to participate actively in the resolution of social dilemmas. Government cannot address all social problems, and federal funding for social programs is being cut at ever increasing rates. According to Lester Salamon, "By forming nonprofit organizations, smaller groupings of people can begin addressing needs that they have not yet convinced others to support." As far back as de Tocqueville's time, it was recognized that the fellowship and support that community-serving nonprofits provide offer individuals a mechanism to accomplish a goal, address a social or political problem, or foster shared values.

In order to remain a viable force for change and service within the community, the nonprofit has to maintain its internal "health." With effective risk management, an organization can continue to be strong, useful, and relevant.

WHAT ASSUMPTIONS MAKE NONPROFIT EXECUTIVES RELUCTANT TO DEVELOP RISK MANAGEMENT PROGRAMS?

Despite the reasons listed above for developing and implementing a risk management program, many nonprofit managers still are reluctant to take the plunge. What nagging fears lurk in their minds and hearts? We call these fears *myths*, and describe them below.

The myths about risk management arise out of one of two assumptions. As members of the nonprofit world — or independent sector — nonprofit executives have been conditioned to believe either (a) that community-serving nonprofits are nothing like for-profit organizations or (b) that community-serving nonprofits must be just like for-profit organizations. Reality is somewhere in between. In terms of operations, clients, and funders, community-serving nonprofits bear little if any resemblance to for-profit organizations, yet nonprofits *do* need to adopt sound business practices in order to survive.

The five primary myths that keep nonprofit executives from undertaking the risk management process are:

1. IT'S EXPENSIVE, TIME CONSUMING, AND COMPLICATED.

True, if you are describing the risk management program developed for an international, multi-faceted organization, but few nonprofits have such complex and risky operations. Risk management programs come in all shapes and sizes. A small, community-serving nonprofit can often develop an effective risk management program through the use of staff and board members in an effort lasting only a few weeks. With some exceptions, there is generally no need to hire consultants, new staff, or put regular programs on hold in order to engage in and implement the risk management process.

Practicing risk management is just utilizing good management and decision-making techniques. The incorporation of risk management into your organization involves taking the time to think about the organization's risks and deciding what to do about them. The process begins by asking and answering three simple questions: (1) What could go wrong? (2) What will we do? and (3) How will we pay for it? As we look at risk management from various perspectives, we will revisit these questions.

Remember our story about Mary's injury from slipping on a wet floor? Doing nothing about risk could be much more expensive and time-consuming in the form of lost time, assets, and negative public relations, then addressing the issues.

2. ONLY LARGE CORPORATIONS NEED A RISK MANAGEMENT PROGRAM.

All organizations, particularly community-serving nonprofits, can benefit from assessing the risks inherent in their operations and policies. Risk management is just as relevant and beneficial to the XYZ Social Services Agency as it is to the largest Fortune 500 corporation, perhaps even more so given the community-serving mission of most nonprofits and the fundamental commitment to protect people from harm.

3. PURCHASING THE RIGHT INSURANCE IS ALL RISK MANAGEMENT INVOLVES.

This may be the most pervasive and dangerous myth about risk management. Insurance is just one method of *financing* risk. Community-serving nonprofits face numerous "uninsurable" as well as insurable risks. In addition, strategies outside a financing arrangement are necessary in the aftermath of an incident affecting a nonprofit's reputation, operations, and viability. An effective risk management program presents proactive strategies for dealing with risk before and after a loss.

4. NO ONE WOULD WANT TO SUE US.

While community-serving nonprofits are rarely sued, when suits and claims are filed, the public relations consequences and the strains on financial resources can be devastating. Regardless of the protection offered by state and federal volunteer protection laws, community-serving nonprofits and their volunteers can be sued — and the costs of defending a lawsuit can be significant. Because community-serving nonprofits have so much to lose in the wake of a crisis, it is crucial that they develop a plan for dealing with risk. The sad story of the AIDS service agency illustrates that an organization can experience the damage of a crisis long after the fact.

5. I'LL HAVE TO READ A LENGTHY MANUAL AND SPEND MONTHS IN BORING CLASSES TO IMPLEMENT RISK MANAGEMENT.

Not unless you've glued *War and Peace* to the back of this guide. There is no reason why risk management needs to be complicated, expensive, time-consuming, or labor intensive. This guide is designed for busy nonprofit executives who have stacks of papers to read, phones ringing off the hook, and, of course, a bare-bones budget.

We've examined the reasons why your nonprofit needs a risk management program, and, we hope, exploded some of the myths about risk management. But how do mishaps and troublesome scenarios actually affect the "nuts and bolts" of a community-serving nonprofit? Read on.

CHAPTER 2

What Have We Got to Lose?

ACTIONS AND (UNANTICIPATED) REACTIONS

For five years, George Smith had served as executive director of ABC Community Service League. A 25-year veteran in nonprofit management, Smith brought to the position impressive credentials, and under his leadership, the League's units of service had grown and the number of grants and corporate gifts received had increased.

Recently, however, members of the board had begun to feel that Smith did not take their concerns seriously or treat them with proper deference. Most members of the board had openly expressed displeasure at Smith's performance — focusing primarily on the executive's relationship with individual board members. As a result, despite Smith's success in guiding the League to new levels of performance and support, the majority of the board wanted to fire him.

But, the board never formally notified Smith that his performance was

unacceptable to the board. The board had never developed performance objectives for Smith, nor had it ever discussed the subject of setting performance goals with its chief executive. The board chair had not completed his most recent performance evaluation. The file consisted of memos to the board chair reflecting individual board members' personal assessments of Smith's performance. While the board was still in the process of crafting a negative performance evaluation, Smith was suddenly hospitalized for complicated cardiac surgery. His prognosis was good, but the doctors projected a three-month recovery.

While Smith was at home recovering from surgery, the board decided to fire him. The board believed that because the executive director, like other League employees, served "at-will," they could terminate his services without liability. The board was not concerned about the consequences of this action, nor was it worried about the potential for negative publicity resulting from the firing of an apparently successful executive whose circumstances would elicit public sympathy.

Did the League's board appropriately weigh its options and consider potential liability before terminating George Smith? Perhaps not. By failing to consider the possible consequences of its actions, the board missed an opportunity to control risk in what may be the riskiest aspect of nonprofit operations — employment relations. The implications of the board's decision to fire Smith could be substantial and long-lasting. We'll come back to Smith a little later in this chapter.

NONPROFIT ASSETS

Assets can be defined as groupings of value, wealth, and benefit — either tangible or intangible. When trouble strikes a nonprofit, the problem is seldom confined to one component of the organization. Four categories of assets are generally at risk in every nonprofit organization. Each of these asset categories can both create exposure and be affected when something goes wrong:

- **People** - Board members, volunteers, employees, clients, donors, and the general public.

- **Property** - Buildings, facilities, equipment, materials, copyrights, and trademarks.

- **Income** - Sales, grants, investment earnings, and contributions.

- **Goodwill** - Reputation, stature in the community, and the ability to raise funds and appeal to prospective volunteers.

For some asset categories, such as property and income, the organization can appraise and assign a dollar value. Other organizational assets, such as

goodwill and people, cannot be assigned a price tag. After all, is it possible to put a price on public trust, or accurately value the creativity of an employee or the capability of a volunteer?

From a risk management standpoint, all four asset categories are important. Each helps a nonprofit realize its mission. Since risk is any uncertainty about a future event that threatens an organization's ability to accomplish its mission, any loss of these assets puts the organization at risk. It is therefore important to understand how each asset category is affected when something goes wrong.

Risk management recognizes the interrelationship among these factors and provides a framework for predicting the potential effect on assets when something goes wrong. Let's revisit the case of George Smith for a closer look. When the ABC board fired George Smith, three categories of assets were in jeopardy:

- *People* - In light of its recent actions, the future viability of the board is in question. Furthermore, the organization's ability to retain the highly competent staff recruited by Smith may be in jeopardy.

- *Income* - As the League's principal fund-raiser, Smith personally raised 70 percent of the agency's $1 million annual budget. Will past donors continue to support the organization following Smith's departure? Also, if Smith sues for wrongful termination, what will be the cost of defending the organization and possibly paying an award?

- *Goodwill* - During his years of service with the League, Smith successfully raised community awareness about the agency's programs, spurring an increase in the number of volunteers. When prospective volunteers read in the local paper about Smith's illness and subsequent termination, will their interest in the organization and enthusiasm for its charitable enterprises wane?

Another example of the interrelationship of these asset categories is the case of the community AIDS organization described in *Chapter One*, which lost a large government contract because it failed to install internal financial controls. The accompanying negative publicity caused an erosion in the organization's donor base and a sharp decline in fund-raising proceeds. As an internal restructuring became necessary, the organization laid off a large number of staff — some with five or more years of service. In addition, the mandated partnership with another AIDS service provider that saved the organization also forced the elimination of some of its programs. The initial cause of the crisis may have been a lack of internal financial controls, but the scenario had dire implications for every category of the organization's core assets.

AT THE HEART OF THE MISSION — PEOPLE

An organization's people are its most essential asset. Any degradation of goodwill or damage to an organization's reputation can make it difficult for a nonprofit to recruit and maintain effective board members, employees, and volunteers. In addition, through their actions, everyone associated with an organization can minimize or increase the risk to all four of the organization's asset categories.

THE BOARD OF DIRECTORS

Nonprofit boards traditionally fulfill the critical role of governing the organization. The board makes policy and is the center of power and responsibility within the nonprofit. The organiza-

tion's bylaws set forth the rules under which the board is expected to operate. As the governance mechanism for an organization, the board sets the direction of the nonprofit and is ultimately responsible for the organization's policies, procedures, and conduct.

people

Because of its critical role as an organizing and oversight body, a nonprofit board truly bears responsibility for the organization's survival. To fulfill this responsibility, the board must discharge its duties as required by law and act to conserve and protect the assets necessary for the organization to survive.

The law requires board members to discharge their responsibilities with the care that an ordinarily prudent person would exercise under similar circumstances — a standard that applies to the actions of for-profit as well as nonprofit boards of directors. The "ordinarily prudent person" doctrine is not prescriptive, nor does it define acceptable and unacceptable board conduct. Instead, the doctrine provides an overall framework for the legal duties of a board member. These legal requirements encompass three areas:

• *The duty of care* generally requires that the director participate actively in the life of the board. Directors are expected to attend board meetings regularly, stay abreast of key developments and matters affecting the nonprofit, and exercise independent judgment in decision-making.

• *The duty of loyalty* requires that a board member give undivided allegiance to the nonprofit when making decisions affecting the organization.

• *The duty of obedience* requires that a director be faithful to the nonprofit's mission, and act in a manner that is consistent with the mission and goals of the organization.

The board can take a number of steps to ensure that its governance activities do not place an organization at risk. Some of these strategies include establishing procedures for meetings (including taking minutes), effectively orienting and training new board members, adopting conflict of interest policies, carefully overseeing financial management and fund-raising policies, and instituting term limits.

NONPROFIT MANAGERS

In many nonprofits, the executive director is the only employee hired by the board. He or she serves as the liaison between the board and the staff or volunteers, the agency and the community, and the agency and those organizations with whom the nonprofit enters into joint ventures. The executive director manages the implementation of initiatives and the administration of policies established by the board of directors.

The executive director's actions or inactions can place a nonprofit at risk. In discharging duties ranging from employee relations to client intake to volunteer recruitment, the executive director can manage risks to the organization's core assets by complying with federal and state laws governing the employment relationship, recognizing the potential risks in utilizing volunteers, and applying the appropriate level of screening required for different volunteer positions.

In short, an effective chief executive must be a skillful manager of people and programs, a lifelong student of the laws and regulations under which his or her agency operates, a seasoned diplomat who cultivates commitment and

support from a pool of volunteers, and a goodwill ambassador capable of developing strong support for the nonprofit in the community.

EMPLOYEES (PAID STAFF*)

*Note: when we refer to "staff" throughout the remainder of this text, we refer to both the employees and volunteers who perform the work of the organization and carry out its mission.

Employees of a nonprofit carry out the mission of the organization by performing specific tasks and fulfilling the responsibilities described in their job descriptions. Each member of the nonprofit's staff is assigned a role that contributes to the organization's mission, goals, and objectives.

Employees' actions and on-the-job decisions can place an organization at risk. For example, employees who act carelessly in delivering services or harass co-workers leave the nonprofit open to lawsuits. While all employees require some supervision, they also need to be fully aware of acceptable procedures, policies, and practices. High performing employees know what the organization expects of them and understand how their interaction with clients, volunteers, and the public can enhance or damage the agency's image and reputation.

VOLUNTEERS

Volunteers offer their time and talent without financial compensation. For most nonprofits non-paid staff members are essential to meeting community needs, but even uncompensated services have a price. One aspect of the true cost of volunteer service is the potential effect a volunteer may have on the organization's assets.

As indicated previously, nonprofits can be held liable for the actions of their paid and volunteer staff under the doctrine of vicarious liability. Therefore, organizations should structure volunteer assignments and manage the risks associated with volunteer activities carefully. In addition, the possibility of having to terminate volunteer staff members should be accepted as a necessary part of risk management.

When properly trained and supervised, the volunteer workforce within an agency provides valuable contributions. Like paid staff, volunteer staff should receive appropriate training, be informed of agency procedures and policies, and be evaluated on a regular basis in order to minimize the organization's liability for the volunteer's missteps. It is essential that volunteers understand their role within the organization *and how their actions can incur liability for the organization and for themselves*.

Volunteers should also understand that in addition to their specific assignments, they are "goodwill ambassadors" representing the agency to clients and the public. How volunteers conduct themselves while on assignment can either present a positive image or degrade the agency's reputation.

SERVICE RECIPIENTS
Service recipients come to an organization to purchase or receive the goods or services that the nonprofit offers. The specific duty owed to a service recipient by a nonprofit varies depending on the individual's status and relationship with the organization and the status of the caregiver. The courts generally require that nonprofits exercise the care of a "reasonably prudent person" in delivering services to service recipients. The level of care changes and may require special precautions when an organization serves a vulnerable population. For example, a day camp owes a

duty of care to its young campers that is far greater than the duty an adult recreational league owes participants in a community softball league. The courts hold individuals recognized as professionals to a higher standard of care. A growing number of nonprofits offer a range of services provided by paid and volunteer professionals, such as health care workers, teachers, counselors, and attorneys.

In addition to exercising reasonable care to avoid potential injury, nonprofits should also establish clear guidelines on client eligibility. A commitment to confidentiality and client privacy should also be addressed in program procedures. An organization should give service recipients as much information as possible about the program, eligibility requirements, waiver procedures, and, if relevant, maximum length of service.

DONORS
Donors are an invaluable and essential asset to any nonprofit. For many agencies, donors include individuals, government agencies, philanthropic foundations, and private businesses. In many instances, donors are also volunteers or clients. Respecting the needs and expectations of donors is essential to risk management.

Practices that minimize the risk of mishaps involving donors include providing information about the intended use of a donor's contribution, and carefully monitoring the use of fund-raising proceeds to ensure that donors' wishes are met. Additional practices are refusing funds or contributions of equipment or other resources that principally benefit the donor and not the nonprofit, and responding to donor inquiries and reporting requirements in a timely and thorough fashion.

THE GENERAL PUBLIC

The public is a general term that encompasses a range of individuals who might come in contact with the nonprofit while purchasing the agency's goods or services, applying to be clients, or applying to be paid or volunteer staff. The public also includes individuals who come in contact with volunteers and staff on a daily basis — or at the time of a mishap such as an auto accident.

Positive public perception and public trust are fragile assets essential to the viability of every nonprofit. The way everyone associated with the organization treats the public will contribute to protecting this vital asset.

PROPERTY

The organization's property-related assets include buildings, facilities, equipment, materials, copyrights, trademarks, hardware, software, and data. The use of automobiles in service delivery creates a significant area of exposure for a nonprofit. The use of widely accessible databases containing confidential client information places an organization at risk of violating client confidentiality. The sale or rental of a nonprofit's mailing list can result in tax liability for unrelated business income.

Controlling the risk of property loss includes preventing damage from water leaks, vandalism, fire or windstorms, minimizing the likelihood of accidents involving the agency's vehicles, protecting valuables from theft, and securing and limiting access to databases.

INCOME

An organization's income generally consists of sales, fees, grants, contributions, and the proceeds of investments. Each of these income components is at risk in the day-to-day operation of a nonprofit. An unexpected increase in expenses also affects an organization's net income. The costs incurred to recreate a donor database lost to a damaged hard drive plus lost donations reduces your income.

SALES

The types of products and services for sale, and the manner in which an organization conducts sales, could place it at risk. Selling seemingly innocuous products such as toys or key chains could pose a serious risk to the organization if, for example, a child chokes on the object. In some circumstances, revenues generated from sales are subject to unrelated business income tax (UBIT).

GRANTS

Income from grants is often contingent upon the agency's use of the funds for the purpose stated in the proposal. In addition, most grant-making organizations require that grantees adhere to a number of procedures, including the submission of timely reports. An agency's failure to adhere to these conditions can result in the withdrawal of grant funds — even after they have been spent.

CONTRIBUTIONS

According to a recent study commissioned by the Independent Sector — a coalition of voluntary organizations, foundations, and corporate giving programs — more than 85 percent of donations to charitable organizations come from individuals. How a nonprofit solicits donations, records the donations, and interacts with the donors is crucial for cultivating and maintaining a solid donor base.

Each state has adopted charitable solicitation laws that a nonprofit must follow in order to avoid liability. The way the organization records donations and issues receipts could put it in an adverse position with the Internal Revenue Service. Carefully review regulatory provisions and incorporate them into fund-raising procedures.

The board is ultimately responsible for ensuring that an agency handles contributions properly. The board, and in particular the board's development committee, should adopt procedures governing the solicitation of donations, handling of receipts, and diligence in complying with grantor and regulatory requirements.

INVESTMENTS

The importance of sound investment policies and careful oversight of investment practices cannot be overstated. A number of recent scandals involving nonprofit organizations have revealed inappropriate as well as criminal practices in previously well-regarded nonprofits. The results of these scandals have included lasting damage to an organization's reputation and ability to raise funds for service delivery. For more information on protecting fund balances and investments, see *Healthy Nonprofits: Conserving Scarce Resources Through Effective Internal Controls*, available from the Nonprofit Risk Management Center.

GOODWILL

Goodwill encompasses the organization's reputation, stature in the community, and ability to raise funds and appeal to prospective volunteers. Although goodwill is an intangible asset, its benefits are manifested in virtually every activity the nonprofit undertakes.

The effects of eroded goodwill are equally evident: a nonprofit's donor base shrinks; the pool of volunteers diminishes; enthusiasm for board service wanes; recruiting highly competent staff becomes more difficult; opportunities to partner with other nonprofits may be hampered; and obtaining public sector monies through grants or contracts may become difficult or impossible.

In short, maintaining goodwill is essential to a nonprofit's ability to accomplish its mission. A risk management program can preserve an organization's good name and positive reputation by preventing accidents or responding appropriately to any incident.

THE EFFECT ON ASSETS WHEN SOMETHING GOES WRONG

An investment in risk management helps an organization keep all four asset categories as secure and productive as possible. The following examples illustrate why an investment in risk management is essential by indicating the types of threats typically faced by nonprofit organizations and discussing the implications of each threat. We highlight the most significant effects possible in each scenario — but keep in mind that other, smaller threats that arise can be troublesome as well.

I. A STAFF MEMBER OR VOLUNTEER IS INJURED ON THE JOB.

When a staff member is injured on the job, his or her value to the organization may be lost for the duration of the disability. Depending on the injured person's assignment, other colleagues will have to fill in, or the organization may have to hire a temporary replacement. Increased costs for workers' compensation (in the form of higher premiums), overtime for other employees, or the costs of bringing in temporary help increase an organization's labor costs and tie up income that could be used for other projects. If the staff member's injury is due to unsafe working conditions, or other types of negligence on the part of the nonprofit, negative publicity might result and damage the nonprofit's reputation.

2. *A CURRENT OR FORMER STAFF MEMBER FILES A COMPLAINT WITH THE EEOC ALLEGING EMPLOYMENT DISCRIMINATION.*

If the accuser is a current employee, this person will be under a great deal of stress. Productivity will suffer, not only for the employee, but also for the person's co-workers and others in the agency. The organization will have to spend funds to investigate and possibly defend the allegations — again reducing the money available for service delivery.

3. A *NONPROFIT FAILS TO ADHERE TO CONTRACT SPECIFICATIONS IN A COLLABORATIVE VENTURE WITH A PUBLIC SECTOR AGENCY.*

In order to obtain funding, most nonprofits enthusiastically agree to meet a funder's conditions and stipulations. By accepting the funding, or promise of funding based on service delivery, the nonprofit agrees contractually to supply certain information or provide services in a prescribed manner. Failure to live up to the spirit or letter of the agreement may put the nonprofit in a state of noncompliance. In many cases, the nonprofit's failure to perform according to requirements is unintentional. The reason may be that the organization is trying to do too much with too few resources. Another reason could be the significant organizational and cultural differences between a nonprofit and a public sector agency —

what would appear to be compliance in the eyes of a nonprofit may be viewed as noncompliance by a funder.

There is a high price for noncompliance. The outcome, even if the media doesn't report it, can damage the goodwill between the nonprofit and the public sector agency. Due to the public nature of the contract, it is always possible that the media could cover the incident, thus damaging the reputation the nonprofit enjoys in the community. Board members, nonprofit executives, and project managers could be held accountable, sometimes publicly, for failing to meet contract stipulations. Damage to professional reputations may result. Even if the staff members are retained, the ordeal could have a long-term affect on their effectiveness. The effect on income could take the form of payments being suspended, penalty fees being imposed, or even the contract being dissolved.

4. A *CLIENT IS INJURED THROUGH A VOLUNTEER'S NEGLIGENCE.*

The total effect on a nonprofit's assets under this scenario could vary considerably based on the nature of the injury sustained (for example, cuts and bruises versus permanent disfigurement). However, under most instances, the principal people affected would be the client(s), the volunteer(s), and the staff member(s) responsible for supervising the activities in question. In addition, this situation involves the board and executive director because they are responsible for establishing and carrying out organizational policies that protect clients' safety — including the recruitment and supervision of volunteers. Supervising volunteers is not simply the purview of a designated staff member. Policies relating to the recruitment, training, and supervision of volunteers are guided by the board's vision and the executive director's administration of board policy.

If the injury results from an automobile accident or from the operation of equipment such as a wheelchair ramp on a van, the nonprofit's property could also be damaged through the volunteer's carelessness or lack of training. If the incident generates negative publicity, or demonstrates that the organization is in violation of a contractual agreement, income could be affected as well. Any type of publicity on such an incident would erode the organization's goodwill in the community. Prospective clients' confidence about their well-being when entrusted to the care of the organization's volunteers may wane. Recovery of the confidence of clients and their families may take many years.

5. A SOCIAL SERVICES AGENCY SERVING FAMILIES IN THE MIDWEST SUFFERS SUBSTANTIAL DAMAGE FOLLOWING A FLOOD.

In this case, the damage may extend beyond the nonprofit. If the flood engulfed the entire region, the agency, its employees, volunteers, clients, and supporters may all be victims. As for goodwill, the agency may be a hero if it continues to provide services or the media and public may accuse it of failing when the community needs its services most. The disaster may also affect the agency's employees, board members, and volunteers personally. They are dealing with the emotional distress of losing their homes and belongings while trying to meet the needs of clients. The emotional toll is even higher if a staff member is killed or severely injured during the flood.

The flood damaged or destroyed the agency's physical assets — equipment, computers, data, and supplies. After a natural disaster, equipment and supplies shortages exist and delay the recovery

process. Expenses increase as the costs of building supplies, labor and other materials rise from the high demand and short supply. The organization's finances are further affected by individuals being unable to give due to their own losses and suffering. Local business support may decrease as businesses recover from the flood. Consequently, when the community's need for services may be at its highest level, the agency may be unable to meet the demand. The agency's ability to recover is affected by the extent of its contingency planning. If the nonprofit developed a disaster recovery plan, the staff is prepared to respond to an emergency and to protect all of the agency's assets.

LESSONS LEARNED

You may regard the above scenarios as unlikely or unnecessarily grim. Unfortunately, they reflect incidents that have taken place in nonprofit organizations throughout the country. These scenarios offer lessons that make a strong case for risk management.

TO BE EFFECTIVE, INDIVIDUALS AT ALL LEVELS WITHIN AN ORGANIZATION MUST UNDERSTAND AND EMBRACE THE RISK MANAGEMENT PROGRAM. OFTEN, AN ORGANIZATION MUST RAISE ITS CONSCIOUSNESS TO ACHIEVE THIS GOAL. A risk management program considers the broad implications of each potential risk on the organization's ability to raise funds, recruit volunteers, protect property, and maintain its good reputation by preserving public trust.

Each problem scenario affected people. Many of the problems cited were exacerbated because the employees, volunteers, management, and board did not understand their core responsibilities for preventing harm and conserving assets. These individuals also did not understand their roles in the nonprofit's overall risk management program.

Perhaps a better understanding of risk management could have prevented or at least modified the severity and ultimate impact of some of these scenarios. Although the implementation of a risk management program will not completely eliminate the potential for accidents or misfortune, risk management can help prevent or minimize many mishaps.

PUBLIC TRUST IS A MIRROR OF THE ORGANIZATION'S HEALTH AND COMPETENCE.

When a nonprofit loses the public's trust, something is very wrong. The source of the dysfunction could be systemic, mission-related, or staff-related. The organization's values could have become corrupted over time or suddenly, because of the handling — or mishandling — of a crisis situation. Whatever surface reasons appear to be the cause of eroding public confidence, there are always problems that lie deeper within the organization.

THERE IS NO SUBSTITUTE FOR A SOUND RISK MANAGEMENT PROGRAM.

We hope that the reader drew this conclusion after perusing the first few scenarios. In each instance, a variety of risk management activities could have mitigated the terrible effects of a mishap.

In *Chapter Three*, we will examine risk management techniques and describe the steps a nonprofit organization can take to create a risk management program. Developing a risk management program can be easier and much less expensive than you think. *Not* developing a risk management program can leave your nonprofit open to tragic consequences that can be avoided. When it comes to risk management, inaction is truly the most expensive option.

CHAPTER 3

How Can a Nonprofit Control Risk?

In *Chapter One*, we defined risk management as a discipline for dealing with the possibility that some future event will cause harm. The primary purpose of a risk management program is to provide an overall approach for dealing with any threat an organization might face in fulfilling its mission. This chapter offers a "blueprint" for an effective risk management program.

ORGANIZING THE RISK MANAGEMENT EFFORT

You can develop an effective risk management program through four general tasks. The first three tasks described below put into action an organization's commitment to and investment in developing the program. The fourth task encompasses the risk management process itself, four steps that will result in a workable, meaningful risk management program tailored to your organization's needs.

A. Establish risk management goals and policy.

B. Assign responsibility for the program.

C. Establish a work plan or timetable for developing the program.

D. Follow the four steps of the risk management process to create the program.

Mission Accomplished: The Workbook leads you through the process of creating a risk management program for your organization. *The Workbook* includes instructions, forms, and checklists.

Some helpful hints:

■ ***Do not postpone the project until the beginning of the next fiscal year***. The first risk management program you develop should address the most probable or volatile areas of risk, so start working on it right away. After all, this plan could be the key to your organization's survival. Once the process is in place, the risk management committee should design the program for one fiscal year at a time — and repeat it each year.

■ *Be realistic — and keep things in perspective*. Beware of paralysis by analysis. Tackling an overly ambitious list of risk management projects in any given year can be overwhelming and result in abandoning this essential project. By establishing priorities for the risks your organization faces, you can develop an "A" and a "B" list of projects. Since risk management is an ongoing process, you can address the projects successively. Each year, the committee should evaluate what it needs to accomplish in the current and succeeding years. The purpose of your *first* risk management project is to begin a continuous process. The first year's risk management plan will not be as complete and refined as the plan produced two, three, or five years from now. What is important is to begin now.

A. ESTABLISH RISK MANAGEMENT GOALS AND POLICY.

The first task is to establish the goals for your organization's risk management program. By initially establishing goals, your nonprofit can determine the steps necessary to achieve them. In addition, goals enable the organization to evaluate the results and effectiveness of its risk management program. The executive director, in collaboration with the board of directors, sets the tone and establishes the agency's risk management goals.

With risk management goals in place, the board of directors, with the executive director, should establish the organization's risk management policy. A risk management policy is a brief (one or two-paragraph) statement of the organization's commitment to risk management. Devising a policy is simple. The Nonprofit Risk Management Center's publication *No Surprises* offers the following sample risk manage-

ment policy: "Brother Joe's Soup Kitchen is committed to practicing effective risk management to protect the safety, dignity, and legal rights of others as well as our human, financial, and intangible assets."

B. ASSIGN RESPONSIBILITY FOR THE PROGRAM.

After adopting a risk management policy, the board and executive director need to designate an individual or team of individuals who will be responsible for developing and, with the board's approval, carrying out the organization's risk management program. While the committee has the primary responsibility for the risk management program, a nonprofit must integrate its commitment to risk management into all levels of the organization.

Risk management is *everyone's* responsibility, so everyone needs to understand and accept the organization's expectations for safe behavior and individual responsibility. The more that people are involved in the process, the greater the chances that risk management will rapidly become institutionalized.

In particular, the key personnel of a community-serving nonprofit have an important role in the risk management process. These individuals can lend specific expertise to the tasks of identifying, prioritizing, and selecting appropriate risk treatment actions. Their advice ensures that the process is focused and efficient.

Board members, employees, and volunteers can staff the risk management committee. Since the risk management program encompasses all aspects of the organization, the committee can divide individual risk management tasks among people in the various operations of the organization. For example, subcommittees — or task forces — can focus on the risks associated with programs (service delivery), fund raising, administrative operations, and the board.

The overall committee supervises the development of an integrated risk management program by coordinating the subcommittees' efforts. The risk management committee also develops the materials and designs the in-service (in-house) training program(s) that will introduce risk management to the organization's board, staff, and volunteers.

C. ESTABLISH A WORK PLAN OR TIMETABLE FOR DEVELOPING THE PROGRAM.

Use the following milestones within your work plan:

- The board adopts a risk management policy.

- The executive director and board develop risk management goals.

- Staff the risk management committee, select its chair, and staff the relevant subcommittees and task forces.

- Set a timetable for specific tasks to achieve risk management goals — including assignments and decisions to be made.

- Set a target date for the completion of each year's annual plan.

- Identify a start date for work on next year's risk management program.

D. FOLLOW THE FOUR STEPS OF THE RISK MANAGEMENT PROCESS TO CREATE THE PROGRAM.

The four steps shown in *Illustration 1* are crucial elements in the development of a risk management program for your organization:

(1) Acknowledge and identify risk.

(2) Evaluate and prioritize risk.

(3) Select and implement risk management techniques.

(4) Monitor and update the risk management program.

Risk Management Cycle

acknowledge and identify risk

evaluate and prioritize risk

implement risk management techniques

monitor and update the program

Illustration 1

Remember, no risk management program can do away with risk altogether. Accidents will happen, and people will file frivolous lawsuits and make unsubstantiated claims. However, an effective risk management program can prevent these circumstances from hurting your organization. Having the appropriate documents and written policies and procedures in place help an organization to prevail in insidious actions.

Documents related to risk management, such as policy statements or procedures, need not be elaborate. Simplicity is the key. If your organization does not have an employment manual, for example, you don't need to create a 500-page tome overnight — or ever. Instead, determine which issues present the most significant and immediate risks, such as hiring and termination policies, and address these first. Then add items as needed.

THE RISK MANAGEMENT PROCESS

STEP 1: ACKNOWLEDGE AND IDENTIFY RISK.

The first step in managing risk is to do some brainstorming to identify risks relevant to your organization. At this point you answer the question: *What can go wrong?* Some generic risks — such as someone slipping on a wet floor or an allegation that the organization engages in unfair labor practices — are present in virtually any organization.

Dimensions of Risk

Illustration 2

Other risks — such as injuries to clients, copyright infringements, or an employee stealing the proceeds of a fundraiser — are unique to certain organizations. No matter how farfetched the possibility seems, if you could envision it happening to your organization, include it in your list of identified risks.

One way to identify risk is to consider the four major dimensions of risk. As depicted in *Illustration 2*, these dimensions include all aspects of the organization. A nonprofit may suffer a loss, adversely affecting its ability to achieve its mission, in any of the dimensions.

1. ***Operational*** — Operational risks are similar to the asset categories (people, property, income, and goodwill) discussed earlier. The loss of *personnel* through disability, death, retirement, or termination can be devastating to a nonprofit. *Physical damage* to its property and the property of others can interfere with the provision of services and be costly. Often, physical damage leads to *consequential* losses whereby, due to a fire at the main office, the agency is unable to operate, loses its funding, or increases its expenses. *Criminal* activity by a volunteer, employee, board member, or client can create a direct financial loss or generate a public relations nightmare. Lastly, the loss of *data* will hamper the agency's ability to fulfill its community-serving mission.

2. ***Legal*** — This dimension includes (a) contractual liability (risks assumed by a nonprofit through formal agreements), (b) statutory liability (those imposed by law), and (c) tort liability (the risks of damage imposed by a private or civil wrong).

3. ***Financial and Market*** — This dimension addresses the business risks that a nonprofit faces, the risk of harm due to changing financial and market conditions. Although an organization cannot control the financial market, it can take preventive measures to protect itself from the market's volatility. Nonprofit managers must exercise care in *investing* financial reserves wisely. Many nonprofits have an investment policy as a guide. Investments may also avoid a

dependence on a single source of funding. *Interest rates* affect the cost of doing business by increasing costs if a nonprofit buys equipment or supplies on credit. *Banking* risks include the financial strength of the banking institution and the nonprofit's relationship with its bank. Many nonprofits lost funds in the savings and loan crisis of the 1980's by placing their funds with banks that eventually collapsed. Lastly, *credit* risks address the availability and costs of credit which are interrelated with interest rates.

4. ***Political*** — Political risks are a large risk factor today with devolution, welfare reform, changing tax laws, and costly regulatory requirements. Most nonprofits are affected by federal, state and local laws and regulations from charitable solicitations to reporting requirements. One new law can dramatically affect how a nonprofit operates. Social action, such as the American public demanding accountability from its nonprofit organizations, is altering how many agencies operate.

A second way to facilitate the identification of risk is to divide the organization into its different operational areas. The following are some possible groups:

■ ***Programs*** — Review the different core programs offered by your agency. If you have varied programs, you can further divide the task of identifying risks by assigning a small group to each program. When examining programs for potential risks, do not forget special activities such as field trips or the annual meeting.

■ ***Fund raising and special events*** — Fund raising presents its own unique set of risks. Special events often create unusual and significant risks that you can easily overlook when examining your organization's day-to-day

operations. *Managing Special Event Risks: 10 Steps to Safety*, available from the Nonprofit Risk Management Center, offers insight into these unique risks.

■ ***Administrative operations*** — A nonprofit's administrative operations may appear innocuous; however, office operations can generate large losses. The administrative subcommittee should focus on the physical facilities, office policies and procedures, employment practices, computer equipment and data, and accounting and financial activities. *Note:* the subjects of management and accounting controls for nonprofits are addressed in *Healthy Nonprofits: Conserving Scarce Resources Through Effective Internal Controls*, available from the Nonprofit Risk Management Center.

■ ***Board governance*** — The board of directors has significant legal and fiduciary responsibilities. Examine the operation of the board including a review of the bylaws, minutes, policies, and procedures.

From your selected groups, examine each operation in light of the four categories of assets (people, property, income, and goodwill) and the dimensions of risk. At this point, identify who and what are at risk. Also, determine what can go wrong and how the accident or event could happen. You should be creative and exhaustive in brainstorming all possible events. For example, for a tutoring program, we can identify the following assets at risk:

✓ *People* - Employees, volunteers, clients, clients' families, the public, vendors (independent contractors), facility owners and their employees (for tutoring sessions at schools, churches, libraries, etc.), board members, and clients' teachers and social workers.

✓ *Property* - Computers and data (client/volunteer databases, tutoring records/progress reports); facilities used for tutoring (schools, churches, libraries, meeting rooms); autos (agency-owned vehicles, volunteer/staff vehicles, field trip transportation); and tutoring supplies (books, teaching aids, and educational equipment, including computers and software, flashcards, puzzles).

✓ *Income* - Consider both revenue (grants, donations, fees) and expenses (salaries, insurance, supplies, rental fees, and recruitment and training costs).

✓ *Goodwill* - Loss of goodwill may occur whenever your nonprofit has an accident or incident. The public's perception of your agency may change after learning of an incident. An effective risk management program seeks to reduce or minimize its negative impact.

TOOLS TO HELP IDENTIFY RISK

Many resources are available to help nonprofits identify and evaluate their risks. Some tools are:

■ *Surveys, checklists, and questionnaires* - Many insurance companies and risk management organizations have developed exposure-analysis forms, which ask for information that will help you identify your risks. Insurance applications also offer some insight into exposures.

■ *Internal documents* - Your agency's own documents and records provide valuable clues to your risks. Review your bylaws, employee manual, audit manual, written policies and procedures, board and committee minutes, staff meeting minutes, internal memos, annual reports, and fund raising/marketing/informational materials to find your exposures.

■ *Financial statements and records* - Financial statements may identify unknown assets and liabilities. A review of financial statements and procedures may also reveal weaknesses in your financial controls.

■ *Workflow* - Map out the workflow and processes used to deliver your services. A visual chart may identify potential problem areas or bottlenecks. The review may include the procedures for a client to sign up for services; the client assignment process; service delivery activities; complaint and grievance resolution procedures; and the monitoring/supervision of staff, volunteers, and clients. Other processes to consider are employment, fund raising, and marketing activities.

■ *Personal inspections* - Many risks cannot be identified by looking at a piece of paper. Inspect all of the offices and facilities used by the organization. Attend the events and program activities to see what is happening and to identify the risks.

■ *Interviews* - Talk to employees, volunteers, staff, donors/grant makers, clients, families or other caregivers, service recipients/customers (clients' employers), and any other people who interact with the agency and its operations. No one knows the risks better than the people doing the job or receiving the benefits.

■ *Loss history* - History often repeats itself unless you take action. Review your agency's incident reports to identify what has happened in the past and detect any trends. In addition, talk with other similar organizations to learn what risks they have identified — this process is called benchmarking.

■ *Similar organizations* - Many risks are common to certain categories of nonprofits, such as recreation programs,

RISK	SEVERITY		FREQUENCY	
	HIGH	LOW	HIGH	LOW
EMPLOYMENT CLAIM	✓			✓
SPORTS INJURIES		✓	✓	

child care centers, programs serving the elderly, and mentoring organizations. One way to identify your risks is to discuss the issue with organizations that offer similar programs or serve similar service recipients.

STEP 2: EVALUATE AND PRIORITIZE RISKS.

The first step in evaluating and prioritizing risks is to estimate the frequency and severity of each risk or exposure.

■ *Frequency* is the probability of each risk becoming reality. The probability estimate examines the likelihood of the event occurring and how often it may occur.

■ *Severity*, in contrast, examines the probable effect on and costs to the organization if the event happens (the potential size of the loss).

Assign a high or low frequency and severity probability grading for each risk. Using a grid, classify each risk by its frequency-severity grading.

Your experience can help you evaluate the frequency and severity of incidents. Examine any accidents or losses your organization experienced. Determine how often each of these types of events occurred each year for the past three years and the cost of the losses incurred from these types of events per year. For example, if your nonprofit owns automobiles or vans used in a transportation program, the following questions could help identify an accident or claims pattern:

■ How often were these vehicles involved in auto accidents?

■ Did the accidents result in any injuries?

■ What was your insurance deductible?

■ Has your auto insurance premium increased because of these accidents? If so, by how much?

■ Was there negative publicity? If so, how did it affect fund raising activities?

If the total number of accidents and related costs are high, then you might assign this risk a high frequency and severity grading. If, on the other hand, auto accidents are rare thanks to good safety procedures, or your nonprofit does not own autos, then the severity or frequency grading for auto accidents will be low.

Using the frequency-severity grid, you can assign priorities to risks. Each quadrant of the grid can be designated as a priority level.

■ Risks graded *high frequency-high severity* can be catastrophic to a nonprofit. These risks should receive top priority. The nonprofit may best be served by avoiding the risk or completely transferring it to another party.

■ Risks graded as *low frequency-high severity* — such as a large property loss, severe auto accidents, or debilitating worker injuries — can happen, and when they do they have expensive consequences. Therefore, these risks should be shared and assigned the next level of priority.

■ The organization can either insure against or retain a *high frequency-low severity* risk (minor auto accidents, liability losses), so these risks are rated as a moderate priority.

■ And lastly, assign the lowest priority to *low frequency-low severity* risks. Your organization can retain the low priority risks, often as a part of an insurance policy deductible.

Focus your actions on the high priority risks that might occur and could prove expensive to your organization, such as a wrongful termination complaint. In contrast, place a lower priority on those risks that are unlikely to occur or that involve an insignificant expense if they do happen, such as a minor theft.

After establishing priorities, evaluate each risk or exposure and select the appropriate risk management technique. A nonprofit can modify any risk, unless it is avoided, to make it acceptable. The next step in the risk management process is to select and implement appropriate modifications and risk management techniques.

STEP 3: SELECT AND IMPLEMENT RISK MANAGEMENT TECHNIQUES.

The selection and implementation phase includes the development of a *brief* written plan outlining how the nonprofit will manage its high priority risks. The plan should address each of the principal risks identified in the previous step and describe the suggested strategy, or combination of strategies, to be employed. The four strategies or techniques for managing risk are avoidance, modification, retention, and sharing (transfer).

AVOIDANCE

A nonprofit can decide not to offer a service or conduct an activity that it considers too risky. This technique removes from the nonprofit the possibility of incurring liability from a specified activity. An example of avoidance is the curtailment of a certain type of client service because the service presents too high a risk exposure for the organization. The potential for this activity to subject the organization to

claims and/or litigation is significant. Therefore, to control this exposure, the community-serving nonprofit chooses to stop providing the service.

Several years ago, a national youth-serving organization decided to remove trampolines from its community-based facilities and therein avoid the risks associated with trampoline use. The organization determined that the recreational benefits from trampoline use were less than the risks of injury and the high cost of training coaches.

Avoidance is a drastic measure. Therefore, less severe alternatives should be carefully considered before deciding to eliminate an activity.

MODIFICATION

An organization can change an activity so that the chance of harm occurring and the impact of potential damage are within acceptable limits. Proper precautions can greatly reduce risk. Modifications can be as simple as training paid and volunteer staff or limiting access to hazardous areas.

Modifying an activity to enhance safety often simply requires the use of common sense. For example, the risk of an auto accident can affect the people, property, income, and goodwill of the community-serving nonprofit. Some risk management-modification techniques in this area include:

✓ Checking the driving records of all drivers (paid or volunteer) and replace unacceptable drivers;

✓ Training all drivers in safe driving techniques, accident procedures and reports, and proper vehicle operation;

✓ Conducting routine vehicle inspections and maintenance, and establishing procedures to report unsafe vehicles; and

✓ Maintaining documentation of risk management activities.

These modification techniques can provide paid and volunteer staff additional information on the organization's expectations of safe behavior and their individual responsibility to act appropriately. The implementation of risk modification activities also heightens the staff's awareness of risk management's role within the organization.

RETENTION

Retention does not mean "do nothing!" It is simply the nonprofit's acceptance of all or part of a risk, including preparing for the consequences by, for example, setting funds aside in a reserve to finance retained losses should they occur.

To determine the size of the reserve funds needed, an organization should forecast the probability of the loss's occurrence — and its probable cost — based on previous experience. Review and update the retention funding plan frequently to decide if the nonprofit should continue to retain the risk, avoid it, or adjust the reserve fund. Retention is a sensible alternative for small losses that will not unduly disrupt operations or affect the nonprofit's financial base.

SHARING

Sharing risk involves the full or partial transfer of an activity — or the financial consequences of a risk — to another party. Examples of risk sharing include mutual-aid agreements with other nonprofits, insurance policies, and contractual agreements that allow a nonprofit to share the responsibility for a risk with another service provider or with a parent who agrees to assume principal responsibility for his child's safety when he signs a participant waiver.

Traditionally, risk management literature calls this option "transfer" because of the presumption that another party would bear the bulk of the risk's financial consequences. Today, however, insurance often includes large deductibles and many limitations and exclusions. Consequently, both parties *share* the financial component of risk.

The role of insurance: The purpose of insurance is to share the financial responsibility for a loss. Because insurance provides an important financial safety net, the nonprofit manager and board should be well-versed in the role of insurance in their operations. The Nonprofit Risk Management Center offers several publications that can help you work through the maze of insurance. Refer to *Chapter Six* for a complete list of resources. In this brief overview of insurance, we will discuss two primary categories of insurance: property and liability.

■ *Property insurance* covers the nonprofit against damage to tangible property such as buildings, computers, furniture, documents, and equipment. Property insurance is also available to cover the expenses associated with reconstructing or salvaging important papers, files, or databases. In addition, property insurance can cover loss of income and the additional expense of setting up an office in another location after a disaster or crisis.

■ *Liability insurance* protects a nonprofit against claims including litigation alleging that the agency's operations or actions caused damage to another person or organization. However, liability insurance does not cover all types of damages, and a general liability policy excludes certain types of lawsuits. A general liability policy will pay the sums the nonprofit becomes legally obligated to pay as damages (including defense costs) for *covered* losses. Most liability policies will pay damages for both economic and non-economic loss, but will not cover punitive damages — "fines" assessed as punishment for grossly negligent or egregious actions. Nor will general liability insurance cover certain types of liability, such as that arising from board decisions or professional liability. Nonprofits can obtain coverage for these potential claims through other policies such as a directors' and officers' (D&O) insurance and professional liability policies.

A community-serving nonprofit requires both property and liability insurance. Sorting out the appropriate types of coverage can be a daunting task. An insurance professional can help the nonprofit manager in determining the best and most cost effective way to share risk.

COST CONSIDERATIONS

An important consideration in selecting a risk management technique is its cost-effectiveness. Resources, especially financial resources, are usually limited in the nonprofit sector. Consequently, you need to determine what your non-profit can and cannot afford — in both dollars and possible negative publicity. The risk management committee should compare the cost of each risk management technique — from avoidance through risk sharing — to its benefits. For example, is the inclusion of "safe driving" in-service training cost effective and beneficial in reducing your risks from automobile accidents, or would the cost be higher than the potential loss?

THE IMPLEMENTATION PLAN

Once the risk management committee selects the appropriate risk management techniques, it should develop an imple-

mentation plan. The plan should document how the organization will implement the selected risk management techniques. The committee should assign responsibilities and the standards that will be used to measure the program's success.

THE RISK MANAGEMENT PROGRAM

The risk management committee should record its actions and plans. The document should summarize all of the nonprofit's risk management activities and the decisions made to accomplish program objectives. What does the document look like? The next major section of this chapter, "The Finished Product," outlines the manual's contents. [*Hint*: The document should bear no resemblance in size to *War and Peace*.]

Although it's tempting to think that completing a risk management program manual means that your work is finished, the reality is that you are only taking a break. Since we are talking about a break, feel free to use this time to take a 15-20 minute coffee break to review the program you have developed. Remember, if you cannot read through the completed risk management program during the coffee break, it's too long.

STEP 4: MONITOR AND UPDATE THE RISK MANAGEMENT PROGRAM.

The risk management committee should review and revise the risk management program at least annually. Nonprofits, like all organizations, are in a constant state of change. Supervising the implementation of the risk management program to ensure it meets changing needs is important. The committee chair should establish a system to collect information and evaluate the effectiveness of the risk management program on a regular basis.

A community-serving nonprofit can experience changes in client needs, service delivery, or available resources. To cope with these changes, the organization must adapt its operations — and the risk management program must change as well. Risk management is a cyclical process. The organization must revisit and update the initial program on a regular basis. We recommend that every nonprofit review its risk management program every fiscal year. An annual review ensures that risk management strategies are relevant, comprehensive, and adequate.

The annual review and evaluation of the current risk management program provides an opportunity to determine if the number of accidents, claims, grievances, or other difficulties has increased or decreased. For example, have injuries from accidents decreased? Has an accident happened in an area not addressed by the risk management program? Has the committee trained the board, staff, and volunteers in risk management? Did issues emerge from the discussions and training sessions that offer clues for other areas that the risk management program should address?

The purpose of the review is not just to capture statistical data. The process gives the nonprofit an opportunity to revisit the significant risk management issues and to determine if the current approach needs major changes or just some refinements.

THE REVIEW PROCESS

A good way to start the review process is to reconsider the three basic risk management questions introduced in *Chapter One*: (1) What can go wrong (that we did not address in last year's program)? (2) What will we do to prevent the harm from occurring, and what will we do in the aftermath of an occurrence? and (3) If something happens, how will we pay for it?

Don't forget to continue managing the risks identified in the current year's program. As risk management becomes institutionalized in your agency, monitoring the program will become a natural part of the overall management function.

THE FINISHED PRODUCT: THE RISK MANAGEMENT PROGRAM

Now that we have examined the risk management process, let us put it together. The risk management committee's activities will culminate in the creation of a risk management manual that documents the components of the risk management program. The manual should:

- Elaborate on the organization's risk management policy and goals;

- Describe the responsibilities of the risk management committee; identify the committee's members and divide the workgroup into appropriate task forces or subcommittees; and set forth the committee chair's job description;

- Briefly explain the committee's process in developing the program and manual;

- List and briefly explain the organization's priority risks;

- Summarize the risk management techniques employed to address the priority risks. The techniques section may refer to other manuals or documents;

- Outline emergency and crisis management plans;

- Describe the process for reviewing and revising the risk management program.

An Important Reminder! The risk management manual does not need to be lengthy. Regard it as the foundation for an effective risk management program for your nonprofit. Completing the first edition of the risk management manual is something to be proud of. A risk management program is an investment in the agency's long-term health and well-being. By developing a risk management program, you have done a service not only to your clients and donors, but also to your paid and volunteer staff. By taking steps to ensure your community-serving nonprofit's viability, you have enhanced the organization's ability to achieve its mission. A worthy accomplishment.

CHAPTER 4

Special Risks Facing Community-Serving Nonprofits

A risk management program outlines an organization's approach to controlling the exposures that put the agency's assets — *people, property, income,* and *goodwill* — at risk. Effective risk management plans address traditional business risks, as well as risks common among nonprofit organizations and risks unique to the particular organization. This chapter focuses on managing the second category of risks — those special risks common in the nonprofit sector. Some areas of nonprofit activity that carry inherent risks include:

- Use of computers, the Internet, e-mail and other tools of the information age.

- Recruiting and supervising volunteers.

- Transporting service recipients.

- Serving vulnerable populations.

- Hosting special events.

- Interacting with the public.

- Administering employment policies.

- Collaborating with others.

- Soliciting and managing restricted funds (grants).

While this is by no means a complete listing, it does cover some of the operational areas that cause the most worry and concern among nonprofit managers — areas where missteps are common and liability may be significant.

The discussion below summarizes the nature of each risk, elaborates on significant risk management issues associated with the activity, and recommends risk modification and risk sharing techniques. We have tried to provide an overview of the kinds of problems that correspond to each activity. Of course every nonprofit is different, so the specific issues or risk modification activities will vary by organization.

As *Chapter Three* illustrated, risk management often involves a combination of tools and techniques. Although any or all of the four principal risk management techniques — *avoidance, modification, retention,* and *sharing* —

---

may be a legitimate option in dealing with the risks discussed below, our discussion will emphasize risk modification techniques and risk sharing activities. The various modification activities recommended for each of the special risks could reduce the possibility of an adverse occurrence or minimize losses if such an event occurs. In particular, insurance is discussed as a common method of risk sharing (transfer).

Just as your risk management program should be efficient and user-friendly, the plan to deal with these special risks need not be elaborate or overly-detailed. A cost-effective plan will emphasize primary risks and develop sound practices to provide adequate protection for your nonprofit.

To cover as much ground as possible, we've kept the discussion for each special risk area deliberately general. As you read this chapter, you should consider how the risk management activities for each of these special risks could best be adapted to fit your organization's needs, size, and focus.

RISKS OF THE INFORMATION AGE*
"To err is human... to really foul things up requires a computer."

In his 1996 book, *Why Things Bite Back: Technology and the Revenge of Unintended Consequences*, Edward Tenner suggested that although technology brings tremendous benefit to modern life, for each advance there are also results that are unexpected. For example, few would argue about the flexibility and ease of travel that arrived with the popularization of the automobile in the 1920s. Yet along with the car came congestion and traffic accidents. Continuing our automobile analogy, air bags have saved thousands of lives, yet have increased the risk of injury to

certain individuals in certain circumstances. One should not forget that even "advances" in existing technologies can have unexpected consequences.

Computers and rapidly emerging information technologies present almost unlimited opportunities but they are also capable of causing a host of headaches. Although few would be willing to give up the rapid communication and access to information that e-mail and the Internet offer, along with these advances come increased risks for nonprofit organizations and a need to identify and manage these risks.

Managing the risks of the information age is a challenge in part because of the rapid pace at which technology is changing. In 1994 there were approximately 15 million Internet users. By the end of 1999 there could be as many as 200 million. In 1997, although much hyped, shopping on the net was considered mostly a "no show", but by 1998 on-line commerce was estimated to have generated sales of nearly $2 billion. The computer and the Internet are changing the way people work, whether we like it or not and nonprofits, as they enter the 21st Century, need to be prepared to deal with the risks of a new information age.

WHAT ARE SOME OF THE RISKS?
The risks brought by use of much of this new technology are as varied as the people in your organization. The risks are easily categorized into property risks, personal injury risks and operational risks. *Property risks* include the possibility of downloading virus contaminated programs or sending and receiving contaminated e-mail messages, any of which can cause loss of files or damage to your own operating systems, software and even hardware. Even more potentially harmful is the

This section is based in large part on a presentation given by Lynette K. Fons in November 1998. It is used here with permission.

damage that results from forwarding contaminated files to others, causing damage to their computer systems. *Personal injury risks* include, but are not limited to, distributing e-mail which may be libelous or defamatory, publication of materials which either invade or disclose private matters for an individual, use of a person's image without consent, disclosure of personal information contained in mailing or other client lists, and risks which are often associated with hard copy publications as they relate to an organization's website. *Operational risks* are those associated with the use of your computers. These include the installation of software without license to do so, use of the organization's computers for illegal purposes or those in direct contravention of the organization's mission.

Specific examples of the risks that can come along with offering access to the Internet in your organization include:

✓ Employees or volunteers using the your computers to communicate with a minor outside of the organization (e.g., solicit sexual favors, sell drugs);

✓ Employees or volunteers communicating with a minor identified through electronically stored information from nonprofit files (e.g., stalking, harassment);

✓ Introduction of computer viruses or damage to the organization's software or equipment.

✓ Unauthorized access to private or privileged information by employees or those outside the organization.

✓ Loss of valuable information through equipment failure caused by environmental factors.

RISK REDUCTION STRATEGIES AND TECHNIQUES
STAFF SCREENING

One of the first lines of defense against persons abusing computer privileges or any risk associated with persons working for an organization is the organization's screening policy. The organization first creates a job description to identify risks associated with the position, then through the application, reference, and interview processes and the appropriate use of other background information, the organization gains a familiarity with its applicants. This information will help you select the most appropriate applicants.

Consider obtaining information pertaining to past addresses, qualifications, including academic background, training, certifications and licensure, experience, background and interests and if appropriate and permitted, about convictions for criminal offenses. It is also good practice to inform the applicant that the failure to provide accurate information can be grounds for dismissal. More information on good screening practices can be found in the publication, *Staff Screening Tool Kit: Building a Strong Foundation Through Careful Staffing* available from the Nonprofit Risk Management Center.

Unfortunately, one cannot rely on screening only. There is no screening technique that can guarantee that persons prone to harming another or causing other problems will not be hired by your organization. Second, the position to be filled may have minimal contact with children or no authorized contact at all. It may be advisable to prevent persons with a relevant criminal history from spending time alone with your clients. However, it may be impractical to completely limit such person's access to a computer or the Internet.

GET IT IN WRITING: ESTABLISHING A POLICY ON THE USE OF COMPUTERS IN THE WORKPLACE

As a second line of defense, protect a broad range of interests by establishing a policy on the use of computers in the workplace. Put it in writing and follow it. It is important to understand that having a policy that is ignored can be very damaging to an organization involved in litigation. A policy is evidence that the organization identified a risk and even contemplated how to avoid it. Failure to follow your policy may be considered evidence of gross negligence and be used to support an award of punitive damages. What would a jury think if the organization had a policy in place that could have prevented an incident but management failed to adhere to the policy?

Without a written policy, expectations of the employee, volunteer or service recipient may not match your own. A policy can help educate staff and volunteers about proper computer and network use and may deter a variety of inappropriate activities from those that may merely be time wasters to those that are more serious and might subject the user or the organization to liability. The presence of a policy may also assist in disciplining a troublesome employee, volunteer or service recipient.

DEVELOPING A COMPUTER USE POLICY

Computer use policies frequently include provisions concerning:

- *Ethics and etiquette* - Etiquette is the exercise of common courtesy, and obeying the standards of conduct that your employees and volunteers would be expected to follow in the office or in interactions with their peers or associates. Staff should be instructed to be polite and refrain from using vulgar or obscene language in any communication and abide by generally accepted office etiquette.

- *Acceptable use* - Your policy should put the user on notice of, and provide information concerning, what your organization considers to be appropriate business related computer use. The purpose of providing Internet or World Wide Web access will generally be to promote the programs and goals of the nonprofit. What is or is not appropriate use should be a determination of the organization and may vary from organization to organization. For example, some organizations may choose to prohibit use of network capabilities for political or religious messages. Such a restriction would not be appropriate for all groups.

To promote efficiency in your organization and to reduce the likelihood that computers will be used for improper purposes, your policy's basic premise should be that use of the system is to support the communications, research, educational, or other stated goals of your organization. Proper use might include correspondence to donors and service recipients, e-mails that conform to your guidelines, gathering data, and downloading or uploading files to further your programs.

Be aware that acts of vandalism and disruption of computer services may result in civil or criminal penalties. Communicate that vandalism and disruption of computer services is prohibited. Vandalism in the context of computer usage includes, but may not be limited to, the creation or transmission of viruses, corruption or destruction of data or an attempt to harm another user of the network, Web, Internet or computer system. By putting this information in writing, management will be in a better position to discipline an employee, volunteer or service recipient who might be guilty of such activities.

◆ *Use of e-mail* - Make it clear that messages sent as electronic mail and documents created and saved should meet the same standards for distribution or display as if they were more tangible documents or instruments. People often feel they are anonymous when using a computer, or that deleted documents vanish. The speed with which a message can be transmitted often eliminates the "sleep on it" factor that may accompany more traditional forms of communication. The ease of transmission means that a message can be redistributed to a vast number of people whom the author never intended to see it.

Existing rules and policies for written communications and common sense should apply even though the medium is electronic. Only electronic documents that the author would be willing to become available to the public should be created.

E-mails can be forwarded, copied, are hard to permanently delete and can play a prominent role in litigation. In a matter involving solicitation of a child over the Internet, consider the ramifications of having a transcript of the entire interaction. Recreated or undeleted files can also be, and frequently are, used as evidence in cases involving discrimination or harassment.

When creating your computer use policy don't forget to address individual use of e-mail or other network services. Some variation of the following language might be appropriate for your organization:

✓ Use of offensive, threatening or harassing materials or language including racial or sexual slurs or comments or obscene material is prohibited;

✓ Solicitation for outside business ventures, commercial purposes or financial gain is prohibited;

✓ Use of e-mail for any activity prohibited by local, state or federal law is a violation of organization policy;

✓ Attempting to use passwords to access fellow employees files is prohibited; and

✓ E-mail communication for non-business related matters is prohibited. (Some organizations allow use for some neutral communications such as making lunch arrangements or scheduling informal meetings.)

Encourage employees to draft all documents, especially e-mail messages, with the expectation that they may be subject to the scrutiny of a judge or jury at some later date in the context of an adversarial proceeding. Sensitize employees through education to the notion that e-mail is not private and is not an appropriate substitute for private conversation. Those familiar with litigation are well aware that requests for documents are not limited to hard copies of materials found in your files. A computer hard drive may be the subject of a request for information from your organization and even deleted files are subject to being discovered.

WHAT A TANGLED WEB WE WEAVE

With its potential to be seen by millions of people each day and the speed with which it can be changed, your organization's World Wide Website is a wonderful tool for promoting your organization and better achieving its mission. However, the same factors that make the Web so powerful also pose unique risk. The management of a website is often handled in a different way then an organization's other publications. Often responsibility is delegated to a staff member who may have strong computer or technical skills but less publishing or editorial experience. Or the task may be contracted out to a person not familiar with the organization or to a volunteer who "knows about Web stuff." The Internet is often regarded as somewhat mysterious or less formal than a printed publication. For this reason, organizations often do not exercise the same diligence and editorial control that is applied to their traditional publications. Yet ironically, electronic publication has the potential to reach many more readers than printed pieces.

It is important to remember that your website and other information that you post on the Internet is a publication of your organization and should be regarded as such. It should be reviewed and subject to the same editorial and managerial controls as your organization's newsletters, magazine and other communications. If your nonprofit has a publishers liability policy, check to see if it covers electronic publications.

Also be aware that by posting information and images (including your logo) on your website, you make it easier for other organizations or unscrupulous individuals to copy and use your intellectual property and trademarks.

WATCH YOUR WEBSITE

You should monitor your website continuously to make sure that the information that is being posted is consistent with the organization's goals and objectives. If you are using another organization's logo or posting information about them, make sure that you have permission to do so.

Think carefully before posting photographs of or personal information about board members, staff or constituents. Never post pictures of children with identifying or personal information on your website. Even posting personal e-mail addresses on your website could subject you to a barrage of messages.

Even if you expect nothing to have changed, check your website at least once each day to make sure that some hacker hasn't gone in and modified your website as a "prank." Such incidents are becoming more common.

CHECKLIST FOR YOUR WEBSITE

✓ Is all the information accurate, up-to-date, and consistent with your printed publications?

✓ Have you controlled access to your website's content to those whom you wish to have access?

✓ Have you made sure that there is no personal or identifying data about board members or staff and especially children on your website?

✓ Have you contacted your insurance carrier to ask about coverage for liability related to electronic publications?

✓ If you are taking orders, doing surveys, or accepting credit cards through your website, are you satisfied with the level of security in the transmission of that information?

If you remember that the Internet is a powerful publication medium, you can minimize the chances that your organization will run into difficulty as a result of your web presence.

DISPELLING EXPECTATIONS OF PRIVACY

A common misconception is that no one other than the person using a computer terminal will see or know what is taking place on-line, placed in directories, or downloaded. In reality, computer-generated documentation is probably harder to get rid of than documents created by other means, and are therefore subject to being discovered and retrieved by others.

There are not many statutes concerning Internet, e-mail, or computers. Examination of e-mail is governed largely by common law privacy considerations. A common question is whether an employer can read employees' e-mail or monitor their Internet activities. Paid and volunteer staff have privacy rights. However, the trend is to consider the office computer as a tool of the workplace in which the employee does not have a reasonable expectation of privacy.

Employers have considerable leeway in monitoring their employees' interoffice e-mail. Courts have largely ruled in favor of employers who have examined the contents of e-mail messages sent by their employees. However, if personal passwords assigned to the employee by an Internet service provider were used to obtain access to the Internet or if a computer owned by the employee was used a reasonable expectation of privacy is more likely to exist. Remember this when an employee asks to use his or her own computer or personal Internet account in the workplace.

Your written e-mail, Internet and computer-use policy should address proper use and clearly inform the system users that they should have no expectation of privacy relative to matters stored on their computer or e-mails, etc. Informing paid and volunteer staff up front that their computer at the office is not accompanied by a right of privacy in its contents will go a long way toward preventing hard feelings and claims that privacy interests were interfered with or that a termination

was improper due to an improper search. Further, a system user who understands that his computer use is subject to review is less likely to abuse his privileges than a person operating under the misconception or belief that no one is looking.

You may want to incorporate the following language or something similar to it into your organization's computer use policy:

> ABC Nonprofit reserves the right to access, review, use or disclose e-mail correspondence and monitor Internet activity when it has a legitimate reason for doing so. E-mail communication is subject to inspection by management at any time. Abuse of e-mail communications or Internet privileges may result in loss of e-mail or Internet privileges and/or other disciplinary action up to and including dismissal.

Of course, the fact that computer and system users have no expectation of privacy can be a double-edged sword. For example, one can identify which employees or volunteers are spending time in a chat room or wasting time on the World Wide Web instead of doing their work, but this ability to monitor could be evidence that you should have known that an employee or volunteer was misusing the resources of your organization and violating the law.

Decide in advance why and when monitoring will take place and who is going to do it. A decision to monitor should be based upon a legitimate need and be undertaken after providing prior notice to users of your computer network that monitoring will occur. Consent (express or implied) should be obtained from persons whose communications will be monitored.

If your employee handbook or computer policy informs the user that the system will be monitored and that they have no reasonable expectation of privacy, consent to monitor will likely be implied, however it is still a good idea to obtain actual consent in writing. To avoid discrimination and harassment claims, the policy should be applied uniformly. Limit disclosure of the results of any monitoring and provide personal privacy safeguards for information obtained.

SECURITY PROCEDURES

Security procedures fall into two categories, personal security and safety and security related to your organization's electronically stored information. Here too, having polices in place helps on several fronts. By informing system users of the organization's rules and expectations, one can reduce the risk of misuse of the system, and in the event the system is misused, there is nevertheless some evidence of an attempt to avert the problem.

Many organizations utilize a password system to avoid unauthorized access to proprietary and confidential information. This helps limit the unauthorized access, as well as opportunities to use or distribute this information outside legitimate and authorized channels. Employees and volunteers should not disclose their network or e-mail password to others. If it becomes necessary to provide a password to another person in order to solve a computer problem or some other legitimate reason, change the password when the need for the computer access is complete. Employees and volunteers should disconnect from the local network and shut down their computers when they leave their offices.

Your organization may benefit from a policy which serves to clarify the fact that all data in the network, hard drives or on floppy disks is considered property of the nonprofit and not to be copied or removed. Further, it is often appropriate to take the position that it is a violation of policy to access computer files in someone else's user directory or on someone else's hard drive without express permission from the creator of the file or without express permission from someone with authority to give it. Paid and volunteer staff and service recipients should not send e-mails under the name of another without permission.

Because systems have been known to fail and networks crash, as an extra measure of protection for your organization's data, regular and complete backups of the organization's computer files and programs from both individual workstations and any fileservers should be a part of your standard operating procedure.

INAPPROPRIATE INFORMATION AND CHILDREN

Children who use a nonprofit's computers should know the ground rules and what to do if they receive inappropriate information or solicitations across the Internet or World Wide Web. They should be encouraged to avoid inappropriate sites. Children should also be cautioned about exchanging personal information with individuals they meet on-line. They should also be encouraged to tell their parents or supervisors if someone requests a meeting. If a staff member or volunteer learns of inappropriate contact being made with a child, for example, a request for a meeting, this information should be given to parents. Failure to do so could result in a claim of negligence against the nonprofit.

Adequate supervision is critical for children using the Internet. Just as one would not send a child unattended on a field trip, one should also make use of a chaperone or an adult supervisor when children use the Internet while under your care or under your control.

PRODUCTIVITY DISTRACTIONS AND INAPPROPRIATE WEBSITES

Public embarrassment and even legal wrangling sometimes can be avoided by taking measures to limit access to unsuitable or adult sites, and by being aware and reacting to inappropriate use of computer networks. There is, for example, software available that will log sites that computer users access. Consider limiting services used at the office through use of firewall programs. Explore restricting access to chat rooms or specific services, or restricting the content of material received over the Internet by scanning keywords, phrases or text strings or based on the source of the information.

Not all programs to restrict access or limit content are created equally and some might interfere with the work of your organization. Consider your philosophy of management, the recipient of the information (age, job classification, etc.) and context when selecting programs and services that will limit access to information.

OUTSIDE PROGRAMS

Persons using your organization's computers should be discouraged from bringing in personal programs, disks and software for use with your organization's computers. Programs, some e-mail messages, information downloaded from the Web, CDs and disks can introduce viruses and many programs use up valuable computer memory. In addition, duplication or use of some programs may violate copyright laws. At a minimum, any materials brought in from the outside should be reviewed by your nonprofit's in-house

technology guru or an outside consultant before they are installed on your network.

RECORDS RETENTION

Policies for computer use should include guidelines for record retention. If normal procedure requires systematic destruction of old documentation on paper, then why not have a policy in place to deal with electronic information? Keep in mind, however, that information thought to be deleted may be present on backup tapes, sectors of a hard drive that have not been written over and may be recovered by special programs. If you are involved in litigation, or anticipate litigation, you should talk to a lawyer regarding deletion of files. Sanctions and adverse inferences relative to the content of deleted or destroyed materials can result when materials are destroyed while a lawsuit is pending and discovery is outstanding. Remember that retention policies for electronic records are subject to discovery in litigation.

EVOLVING LEGISLATION

Few laws regulate or even reference computers or the Internet. A few laws written before the emergence of the Internet and widespread computer use have been interpreted to apply to crimes that might be carried out with a computer or the World Wide Web. Other laws have been amended to include references to computers. Some attempts at legislation, including those specifically intended to protect minors from being harmed due to their use of the Internet and the World Wide Web have been overturned by the courts due to First Amendment concerns.

In 1996, Congress passed the *Communications Decency Act*, broadening existing legislation that made it illegal to engage in threatening, abusive and obscene communications over the telephone. It provided in part that, "Whoever in interstate or foreign communications knowingly uses any interactive computer service to display in a manner available to a person under 18 years of age, any comment, request, suggestions, proposal, image or other communication that in context, depicts or describes in terms patently offensive as measured by contemporary community standards, sexual or excretory activities or organs... shall be fined under Title 18, or imprisoned not more than two years or both." 47 U.S.C. 223(d).

The United States Supreme Court in *Reno v. ACLU*, declared that while this legislation was designed to limit minors' access to certain materials, the law was too broad and effectively banned certain protected speech among adults. The Supreme Court ruled that the Internet deserved the same high level of free speech protection afforded to books and other printed matter.

Lawmakers in many states are considering legislation to govern computer use and/or the content of electronic transmissions, as is the federal government. However, this is a complex and emerging area and it will take many years for laws to be developed and tested in the courts. Meanwhile technology will continue to move forward and so must we.

Like other business tools, computers and the Internet can bring a new level of efficiency to your organization and help you to deliver services better than ever. Well thought-out policies and procedures and a little common sense can help every nonprofit reap the tremendous benefits of technology, while minimizing the chances of harm to the organization, its staff, and its service recipients.

RECRUITING AND SUPERVISING VOLUNTEERS
NATURE OF THE RISK
Community-serving nonprofits recruit and train volunteers to carry out some or all of the organization's services. Volunteers work directly with clients, staff, management, and sometimes the public. They generally provide services without compensation, although some volunteers may receive educational stipends or other forms of compensation.

Whether laws governing the employer/employee relationship apply in the recruitment and supervision of volunteers depends on whether the *state* considers that an individual is serving as a "volunteer" or an "employee." Generally, employment laws apply to paid staff. Volunteers are usually exempt from coverage by these laws. The label a nonprofit assigns to an individual is not the determining factor in whether that person is considered by the state to be a volunteer or an employee; therefore, your relationship with a "volunteer" in your organization may be subject to employment laws and standards.

Laws that apply to hiring and other employment practices may also apply to volunteers. In general, however, antidiscrimination laws such as the Civil Rights Act of 1964, Age Discrimination in Employment Act of 1967, and the Pregnancy Discrimination Act do not protect volunteers who receive no compensation. The Americans with Disabilities Act of 1990 could apply to volunteers, but only in terms of public accommodations.

Risk management activities in the area of volunteer recruitment and supervision emphasize the need to recruit and train competent individuals whose motivations and willingness to be supervised are within appropriate bounds. When properly trained and supervised, an agency's volunteer workforce can provide valuable contributions to a nonprofit as well as to its clients and the public. Nonprofit managers must ensure that they recruit and supervise volunteers within the parameters of applicable laws and governmental agency regulations. *The Staff Screening Tool Kit: Building a Strong Foundation Through Careful Staffing*, available from the Nonprofit Risk Management Center, offers guidance on establishing an effective screening program.

SAFE PRACTICES FOR RECRUITING AND SUPERVISING VOLUNTEERS

To effectively recruit volunteers, your organization should:

■ *Develop thorough screening policies and procedures.* The cornerstones of a complete screening process are position descriptions, completed applications, and interviews. The depth and type of screening process should be tailored to the degree of risk presented by each position.

■ *Incorporate reference and background checks as appropriate.* Checking an individual's references is appropriate for every position — paid or volunteer. Additional background checks may be warranted based on a prospective volunteer's assignments. For example, conduct motor vehicle records checks on volunteer drivers. A volunteer who will work one-on-one with children or the elderly should be subject to a criminal history records check for relevant convictions.

■ *Adopt privacy policies.* Establish policies and procedures that protect the privacy rights of applicants for all volunteer and paid positions.

■ *Provide new volunteers with a substantive orientation.* Orientation programs for new paid and volunteer staff should include discussions of the organization's mission, performance expectations, disciplinary measures, operational policies, and safety policies.

The effective supervision of volunteers requires that the organization:

■ *Provide clear expectations of performance.* Effective volunteers know what is expected of them and have the skills required to perform the assigned tasks. A job or position description for each volunteer position is a starting point for providing clear direction.

■ *Provide appropriate skill and safety training.* Every nonprofit that involves volunteers has an obligation to provide skill and safety training to ensure that its volunteers have the knowledge, skills, and tools necessary to perform effectively.

■ *Provide procedures for reporting problems or suggesting changes.* Instruct every volunteer about his or her responsibility for spotting and reporting potential hazards that place the organization's resources at risk. In addition, encourage volunteers to participate in developing solutions to problems and challenges that place assets at risk.

■ *Supervise volunteers carefully.* Volunteers at your agency may or may not be accustomed to close supervision and performance stipulations. Occasionally, a volunteer may express the view that anyone who works without pay should not be subject to close supervision. The belief that an unproductive volunteer is better than no help at all is often costly. The organization could incur liability as a direct result of its volunteers' actions or failure to act. Courts throughout the country have held nonprofits liable for the actions of their volunteers in the same way that organizations are held responsible for the actions of their employees. Through proper supervision, the nonprofit can ensure that a volunteer is meeting its expectations and operating under its guidelines. Volunteers also need to understand that their actions can subject the nonprofit to claims or litigation, and that the public often judges an organization based on the behavior of its volunteers.

■ *Develop a grievance procedure.* When volunteers are supervised and held accountable for their actions, a nonprofit should consider providing a means by which these individuals can appeal a ruling they believe to be unfair. Often individuals file claims or institute litigation because they feel their grievances have not been heard by the appropriate people. Many such complaints could be avoided by having a grievance procedure in place. A grievance procedure works to the benefit of both paid and unpaid staff and functions as a safety valve. By deciding in advance how it will handle complaints, a nonprofit can offer volunteers and employees a forum to air and resolve disputes.

RISK MODIFICATION TECHNIQUES FOR RECRUITING AND SUPERVISING VOLUNTEERS

EDUCATION AND TRAINING

Volunteers are frequently the lifeblood of a community-serving nonprofit. As a valuable resource, give your volunteers as much information as possible about the agency's focus, operations, and expectations regarding the performance and behavior of *all* of its staff. Closely supervise volunteers to ensure that they understand their assignments and that tasks are completed in a satisfactory manner. Provide feedback about their progress and performance, and counseling if their work does not meet your agency's expectations. Because nonprofits are accountable for the actions of their volunteers, address inappropriate conduct or other indications of unsuit-

able performance in a timely and consistent fashion. Also, recognize the occasional need to terminate volunteers to protect your agency's scarce resources.

Communication is an important risk modification tool. The orientation offered to new staff is crucial in providing volunteers with an understanding and appreciation of the history of the organization, the work they will be doing, and the nonprofit's expectations in terms of performance, behavior, and public relations. A comprehensive orientation might cover:

■ The organization's history and mission.

■ The population served.

■ Organizational structure, including key personnel.

■ The staff code of conduct, including policies regarding appropriate and inappropriate behavior.

■ Conflict of interest policy.

■ The organization's policies and procedures, including:

  ✓ Volunteer screening program - documentation, tests, ongoing requirements.

  ✓ Confidentiality policy as it applies to volunteers, employees and clients.

  ✓ Supervision and disciplinary policies.

  ✓ Accident response/reporting and crisis management procedures.

■ Job-specific orientation and training, covering:

  ✓ Job or position description.

  ✓ Training requirements.

  ✓ Financial controls.

  ✓ Supervision and chain of command.

RISK SHARING MECHANISMS FOR RECRUITING AND SUPERVISING VOLUNTEERS

INSURANCE

Volunteers create two types of exposures. The first is injury to the volunteer. The second is harm to someone else caused by a volunteer. In both cases, the injured party may allege that the nonprofit was negligent in its duty to protect the safety of volunteers and clients. Different types of insurance policies address these exposures.

■ *Injuries to Volunteers.* An organization has two options to insure volunteers against the possibility of physical harm which occurs in the course of volunteer service: carrying a separate volunteer accident and injury policy or including volunteers under a workers' compensation policy. In some cases, the commercial general liability policy carried by the organization may cover injury to a volunteer caused by the organization's negligence.

♦ *Accident and injury policy.* This type of policy finances the cost of medical treatment for volunteers injured while delivering services for the organization. The policy usually pays the cost of emergency room services and follow-up treatment to pre-determined limits based upon the kind of injury. Organizations can select the limits appropriate to their need and financial resources.

An accident policy does not respond to illness, nor does it protect the organization from liability for the injury. One distinctive feature of an accident policy is that it will pay a claim regardless of who is at fault as long as a covered person suffers an injury. These policies are often excess insurance — which means that the policy will pay only after other available insurance, such as the volunteer's personal health insurance, is exhausted. If the volunteer does not have health insurance, the accident

policy would become the primary coverage for the volunteer.

♦ *Workers compensation.* Some states allow a nonprofit to include volunteers under the organization's workers compensation policy. While this may appear to be an easy answer to the dilemma of providing a source of recovery for injured volunteers, a workers compensation policy may not be the most effective way to protect volunteers. A workers compensation policy provides both medical and indemnity (lost wages) benefits.

The advantage of a workers compensation policy is that the medical benefits are unlimited; however, how do you reimburse a volunteer for lost wages? Is the volunteer compensated on the basis of the actual employment (corporate executive) or the volunteer position (food server at a soup kitchen)? Another problem is developing the premium basis for the volunteers. Workers compensation premiums are usually based on the organization's payroll. How does one calculate the payroll for volunteers? Some insurance companies use comparable salaries, meaning a food server volunteer would be charged based on the average hourly rate for that position. Therefore, the organization may have to keep detailed records of the types and hours worked by volunteers. Lastly, workers' compensation policies are affected by the organization's actual losses through a process called experience rating. With a large volunteer workforce, accidents *will* occur and these incidents can increase premium costs substantially.

♦ *Commercial General Liability (CGL).* Another concern is when the organization is allegedly negligent in injuring a volunteer. A CGL policy may or may not protect a nonprofit from a volunteer's claim. For covered injuries (bodily injury, property damage, personal injury), volunteer injuries are usually covered to the same extent as injuries to clients and members of the public. However, if volunteers are included on the policy as a "named insured" or "additional insured" and the policy includes an "insured vs. insured" exclusion, the organization may not be protected since the volunteer is an "insured" under the policy. Most policies contain a "separation of insureds" provision that provides coverage when one insured files a claim against another insured (i.e., volunteer vs. agency).

Some policies include an endorsement or provision that excludes coverage for claims filed by one insured against another. And some "volunteer - additional insured" endorsements exclude coverage for a volunteer vs. volunteer claim, even if the policy includes the "separation of insureds" provision.

■ *Injuries to Others.* Volunteers, through their negligence, may cause an injury to a client, employee, volunteer, or member of the public. A commercial general liability policy covers a nonprofit for claims arising from the activities of its agents — including employees and volunteers. If the volunteers are included as "insureds" under the CGL policy, the coverage will protect both the organization and its volunteers. Therefore, if the volunteer is named in the lawsuit in addition to the organization, the insurance company will defend both the volunteer and the organization. If volunteers are not "insureds," the individual volunteer would not be afforded coverage by the nonprofit's CGL policy. It is important to review the policy wording carefully and seek advice from an insurance professional if you are uncertain about whether coverage would apply in a particular instance.

CONTRACTUAL RISK SHARING
The sharing of risk through the use of contracts is limited for injuries to volunteers. An organization could require its volunteers to sign a waiver or release of liability whereby the volunteer agrees not to sue the organization in the event of an accident. Such a requirement could discourage people from volunteering. The waiver also addresses only claims from volunteers; it does not help with injuries caused by volunteers.

TRANSPORTING SERVICE RECIPIENTS
NATURE OF THE RISK
Most community-serving nonprofits have transportation-related risks. Even if an organization does not regularly transport its clients, volunteers and employees may occasionally drive on the organization's behalf.

Some nonprofits regularly transport clients to and from service delivery sites, such as emergency shelters, medical facilities, and recreational activities. Ensuring the safety of vehicles, passengers, and drivers is essential to managing transportation-related risks.

RISK MANAGEMENT ISSUES RELATED TO SAFE DRIVING AND VEHICLE MAINTENANCE
The primary issues related to safe driving include:

■ Selection and screening of drivers.

■ Driver training in defensive-driving and emergency measures.

■ Safe driving policies.

■ Driver training for special vehicles.

Vehicle maintenance is a crucial element of managing transportation risks. Even the safest drivers can be involved in an auto accident if the vehicle is in an unsafe condition. Policies that can help to maintain vehicle safety include:

✓ Clear lines of responsibility for vehicle maintenance and repair.

✓ Incident and accident reporting procedures.

✓ Regular transportation safety audits.

RISK MODIFICATION TECHNIQUES FOR SAFE DRIVING AND VEHICLE MAINTENANCE

SELECTION AND SCREENING OF DRIVERS

A nonprofit should verify that all drivers — employees and volunteers — are properly licensed and qualified to drive assigned vehicles. Require all drivers to complete an application that includes questions about moving traffic violations, current or revoked licenses or permits, and types of licenses held. The application should include the individual's permission for the nonprofit to receive his or her Department of Motor Vehicles driving record (MVR). Secure a copy of each driver's license and MVR. A license will identify any restrictions the state has imposed upon the driver, such as the need for corrective lenses, special mirrors, or restricted driving times.

The nonprofit should require some drivers, depending upon their responsibilities, to pass a practical driving test. The road test will confirm safe driving habits, such as fully stopping at stop signs and driving safely on highways and in inclement weather.

TRAINING IN DEFENSIVE DRIVING AND EMERGENCY MEASURES

Offer training courses in defensive driving and emergency measures to all individuals who drive as part of their regular job duties, whether or not the person drives a vehicle owned by the organization. Inviting local or state law enforcement officials to lecture on safe driving can effectively emphasize the need to drive safely at all times.

In addition to safe-driving training, training in what to say and do in emergency situations is important. The heightened emotional reaction that takes place during such incidents can lead to miscommunication — and the potential loss of goodwill. With proper training, the potential for a volunteer or staff member to make a costly mistake at the time of an accident, like declaring that the agency's insurance "will take care of everything," is minimized.

SAFE DRIVING POLICY

Develop written policies on safe driving. The policies need not be lengthy or overly-detailed. A sample driving policy might contain these points:

✓ Use seat belts and headlights at all times.

✓ Submit an annual motor vehicle driving record and pass the agency's road test every three years.

✓ Obey all traffic laws.

✓ Always have your license with you when driving.

✓ Do not consume alcohol or take medication that may impair vision, hearing, or reflexes prior to or while driving for the nonprofit.

✓ Keep doors locked when driving and when the car is parked.

✓ Do not drive if tired or not feeling well.

In addition, a safe driving policy should define an acceptable or unacceptable driving record. For example, the guidelines might be:

An individual will be denied driving privileges if, within the last ten years, he or she has had:

✓ A felony conviction involving a motor vehicle.

✓ A conviction for reckless driving, driving while intoxicated, or driving under the influence.

✓ Two or more moving violations.

✓ A license suspended or revoked.

✓ A conviction for driving without insurance.

✓ Two or more "at fault" accidents.

If a driver fails to meet the organization's performance expectations, remove the person from the roster of approved drivers. This may be a challenge if the driver is a long-term volunteer or board member. However, the consistent enforcement of these policies sends a message to all drivers within the organization.

DRIVER TRAINING FOR SPECIAL VEHICLES

Many community-serving nonprofits own or operate special vehicles, passenger vans or buses, vehicles with lifts, or large trucks. These vehicles may require a Commercial Driver's License (CDL) or other special permit. If your organization owns or uses special vehicles, make sure that the drivers of these vehicles have the required licenses.

Although a vehicle may not require a special license, operating it may necessitate special training. Someone who has only driven private passenger cars may have difficulty adjusting to a van or panel truck. For example, a panel truck has very limited visibility, so the driver is dependent upon the side mirrors — something most people are not used to using when driving. Driving vehicles with lifts, especially for wheelchairs, requires training to ensure their safe operation.

CLARIFY LINES OF RESPONSIBILITY FOR VEHICLE MAINTENANCE AND REPAIR

Assign one person (with a back-up) to be responsible for ensuring that all agency-owned vehicles are maintained and repaired. The vehicle "supervisor" should oversee the maintenance and repair procedures, such as:

✓ *Mileage and maintenance log.* Each vehicle should have a log book for drivers to record each trip, including the driver, purpose, and miles driven. The book should also document any maintenance or repairs performed.

✓ *Pre-trip inspection.* Develop a short pre-trip inspection form to be completed by the driver before using the vehicle. The driver should refer any problems to the vehicle supervisor. The supervisor should also inspect the vehicles periodically.

✓ *Routine maintenance.* Schedule and document the routine maintenance of all vehicles (oil changes, tire rotation and replacement, fluids checked).

✓ *Maintenance or repair requests.* Establish a way for a driver to report maintenance and repair needs (flat tire, dirty windows, broken seat belt).

INCIDENT AND ACCIDENT REPORTING PROCEDURES

Safe driver training should address the procedures for reporting an accident or incident. The report should detail any maintenance or repair needs caused by the incident. All incidents — even those that do not result in damage or injury — should be reported because a "near miss" can offer valuable lessons.

TRANSPORTATION SAFETY AUDIT

The risk management committee and the vehicles "supervisor" should regularly review the vehicles' records and accident/incident reports. The purpose of the review is to determine if the appropriate actions were taken. The committee should modify the transportation safety procedures to respond to any deficiencies.

RISK SHARING MECHANISMS FOR SAFE DRIVING AND VEHICLE MAINTENANCE

INSURANCE

Nonprofits should consider two types of insurance to cover exposures related to motor vehicles. The first is insurance for any vehicles the organization owns or leases on a long-term basis. The second is coverage for vehicles operated on the nonprofit's behalf, but owned by others, including leased, rented, hired, or borrowed vehicles. Any organization that owns or leases vehicles should have a business auto policy (BAP). BAP coverage can include hired and non-owned vehicles.

Unfortunately, many nonprofits that do not own any vehicles do not carry insurance coverage for liability caused by non-owned or hired automobiles. Instead, they rely on their drivers' assurances of maintaining adequate coverage and assume that such coverage will adequately protect the nonprofit from liability. In reality, the drivers' policy limits may be inadequate, or the coverage may be canceled or provided by an insolvent insurance company.

A growing number of nonprofits carry commercial general liability (CGL) policies, but CGL policies often exclude vehicular risks. A nonprofit can purchase an endorsement to include hired and non-owned auto coverage under its CGL policy.

If your nonprofit does not own any vehicles but benefits from the use of cars owned by others, non-owned/hired auto insurance is a must. Non-owned/hired coverage is generally written as excess over any collectible insurance — including the driver's personal auto coverage. Many insurers will offer hired and non-owned auto coverage as part of an overall insurance package that includes property and general liability coverages.

Every organization needs to pay close attention to how its insurance policy covers its drivers. Some insurers require a list of drivers, underwrite each driver, and then exclude any unacceptable drivers and all other non-scheduled or unlisted drivers. Other insurers may cover employees, but exclude volunteers. Each organization must carefully examine its insurance policies to ensure that its unique situation is addressed appropriately.

CONTRACTUAL RISK SHARING
One strategy for sharing the risk with another organization is to contract with a commercial driving service. However, there are many issues to consider when dealing with a contract service.

First, an organization can be held liable for negligently selecting a commercial transportation service. Each organization should establish and document its vendor selection process. The selection review should include information about the company's driver training and qualifications, vehicle inspection and maintenance procedures, and the company's operating authority and history of compliance. Check company references, business history, and insurance coverage.

As is appropriate with any vendor engaged by a nonprofit, a commercial transportation service should agree to indemnify the nonprofit against any claims that result from the services the vendor provides. The contract with the vendor should specify that the vehicles used by the contractor will meet or exceed all applicable safety requirements and that the drivers are qualified by training and experience and are licensed to operate the vehicles used. Any failure by the vendor to comply with these provisions should constitute a breach of contract and empower the organization to void the contract immediately.

To ensure that the coverage purchased by the commercial service will cover the nonprofit, many organizations insist that they be named as an additional insured on the vendor's commercial automobile policy. This may not be necessary due to the "omnibus clause" contained in the standard Business Auto Policy. The omnibus clause broadens the definition of "insured" to include "anyone liable for the conduct of an insured." This clause has been interpreted to include the customers of a commercial transportation service. Before relying on this provision, however, verify that the vendor's policy contains the omnibus clause.

A nonprofit should also determine whether the commercial transportation service carries "adequate" limits. "Adequate" will depend upon the type and size of the vehicle. A $1 million limit may be acceptable for a private passenger car, but it is probably unacceptable for a 44-passenger bus. Request a certificate of insurance to confirm adequate limits.

Once the contracted services have been initiated, the nonprofit should monitor the vendor's compliance with the contract terms. Monitoring might include requiring vehicle inspections, requesting feedback from passengers, and requiring proof of adequate insurance coverage.

SERVING VULNERABLE POPULATIONS
NATURE OF THE RISK
Vulnerable populations include those individuals who, because of their age or physical or mental impairments, are at risk for abuse, coercion, or intimidation by another. These populations include but are not limited to children, the elderly, individuals with developmental or physical disabilities, and persons recovering from substance abuse.

Nonprofits that serve vulnerable populations have a special obligation to take extraordinary care in protecting service recipients. Managing these risks begins with recognition of the risks involved — such as neglect, abuse, or malpractice — on the part of the organization's paid and volunteer staff. Clear communication is essential to maintaining a climate of trust among the agency, the clients, and the clients' caregivers.

RISK MANAGEMENT ISSUES RELATED TO SERVING VULNERABLE POPULATIONS
The risk management issues central to working with vulnerable populations include:

■ *Screening and selecting paid and volunteer staff.* The potential for abuse and mistreatment of clients is usually associated with insufficient hiring practices or lax supervision of employees and volunteers. Careful screening and appropriate documentation are crucial in making good staffing choices for both paid staff and unpaid volunteers. An organization can be held liable for selecting and retaining an employee or volunteer who is incompetent or unfit. The determination of whether a hiring decision is indeed "negligent" rests on what the organization knew, or should have known, when making its selection decision. The courts ask whether, given the circumstances, it was reasonable to select that individual for the position.

■ *Training and supervising paid and volunteer staff.* Negligence in supervision is another area in which the organization can incur liability. As mentioned earlier, the courts have established the nonprofit's responsibility to set clear boundaries of acceptable behavior for staff. Careful monitoring and supervision of volunteers and employees working with vulnerable populations is essential in minimizing the organization's liability.

■ *Legal requirements — reporting child abuse or neglect.* All fifty states have enacted abuse and neglect reporting legislation. This legislation obligates professionals and often others to report abuse or neglect. Although most of the legislation is primarily focused on protecting children, many states have enacted similar laws for other vulnerable populations. Regardless of the laws, it is important to monitor the organization's clientele to ensure that no abuse or neglect is taking place.

■ *Crisis management — handling allegations of abuse and other inappropriate conduct.* If neglect or abuse is discovered, the organization must be prepared to deal with the repercussions. The staff must know how to report its suspicions and what to do after that. Many nonprofits incorporate the reporting of suspected abuse in their crisis management plan.

RISK MODIFICATION TECHNIQUES FOR SERVING VULNERABLE POPULATIONS

SCREENING AND SELECTION
The careful screening and selection of employees and volunteers is one of the most important ways to reduce the possibility of abuse or neglect. An effective screening and selection process includes the use of:

✓ Position descriptions.

✓ Comprehensive reference checks.

✓ Face-to-face interviews to probe for abusive tendencies.

✓ Orientation and training to explain the organization's policies.

For additional resources on screening and selection, refer to *Staff Screening Tool Kit: Building a Strong Foundation Through Careful Staffing* and *Child Abuse Preven-*

tion Primer for Your Organization. Both books are available from the Nonprofit Risk Management Center.

TRAINING AND SUPERVISION
The quality and frequency of training both reinforce the nonprofit's policies and further develop everyone's understanding of the clients' physical and emotional development. Training can ensure that the employees and volunteers understand how to avoid being placed in compromising situations. For example, institute a buddy system to ensure that at least one colleague is nearby at all times and insist that interaction with the client be in the open.

Training is also a way to determine that an individual is competent to perform the assigned tasks. Be clear about the type of work the person will be doing, the degree of supervision provided, and the safeguards that are in place. Clearly express the organization's mission, activities, and acceptable practices, and adopt written policies that clearly prohibit unauthorized conduct. Educate staff about what is appropriate and what is not. Define the conduct or activities deemed to be unacceptable or permitted only with prior organizational and caregiver approval; articulate the organization's "zero tolerance" position.

LEGAL REQUIREMENTS
Know your state's abuse and neglect reporting requirements. Identify which vulnerable populations are protected, who must report suspected cases, and to whom the incident must be reported. Establish internal procedures for reporting and investigating suspected abuse or neglect. Remember that the abuse or neglect could be caused by an employee, volunteer, or client of the nonprofit — or by someone outside of the organization.

CRISIS MANAGEMENT

Establish procedures for reporting problems. Volunteers, employees, and caregivers should each have a means to bring problems to the attention of management for a *quick* resolution. In the event of an adverse incident, the nonprofit should handle the allegations and accusations in a manner that is considerate of the client and others. Address the allegations in a confidential and caring manner, and work cooperatively with the organization's legal counsel.

Another aspect of crisis management is dealing with the media when the allegations become public. Every nonprofit should have a designated spokesperson (and back-up) trained in media relations. Refer to the "Interacting With the Public" section of this chapter for additional information on working with the media.

For additional information on crisis management, refer to *Crisis Management for Nonprofit Organizations: Ten Steps for Survival,* available from the Nonprofit Risk Management Center.

RISK SHARING MECHANISMS FOR SERVING VULNERABLE POPULATIONS

INSURANCE

Commercial general liability (CGL) policies cover the organization for bodily injury and property damage claims from a third party. Clients, volunteers, or the public may submit a claim against a nonprofit. An organization's policy may or may not include volunteers as an "insured." (Refer back to "Recruiting and Selecting Volunteers" for a discussion of volunteers as "insureds.")

Most commercial general liability policies exclude coverage for abuse or molestation claims because abuse or molestation is an intentional act — the abuser intentionally harmed another person — and the CGL policy excludes intentional injuries. The second rationale for the exclusion is that neither abuse nor molestation fit the policy definition of "bodily injury." A nonprofit can purchase coverage for abuse or molestation claims either as an endorsement to the CGL policy or in a separate policy. The coverage will protect the organization, but it may not extend to the person who perpetrated the abuse or molestation if he or she is convicted.

Directors' & Officers' Liability insurance (D&O) covers the errors and omissions or wrongful acts of the organization's board of directors. A board's responsibility is one of governance; consequently, claims have been filed accusing a board of neglect in its duty to govern and protect properly the nonprofit's clients. Therefore, abuse and molestation claims have been successfully filed under D&O policies. Some insurance companies, in response to these claims, have added an abuse exclusion. Check your policy carefully to determine if the policy would respond to an abuse-type claim. Also, make sure that the policy will protect the organization and its directors, officers, employees, and volunteers.

HOSTING SPECIAL EVENTS
NATURE OF THE RISK

Special events are occasions that involve activities beyond the normal operation of the organization. Often these affairs are fund-raising activities or events to increase public awareness of the nonprofit's mission and services. Pre-event publicity and media coverage of the actual event may heighten the organization's visibility.

Special events can take place at the nonprofit's usual place of business or at another location. The nonprofit invites the public to attend these events, and often charges an admission or other fee. In some cases, the festivities include serving alcoholic beverages and gaming entertainment.

RISK MANAGEMENT ISSUES RELATED TO HOSTING SPECIAL EVENTS

Special events, by their nature, are a departure from the organization's normal operations. The circumstances associated with the events, such as the inflow of cash or other valuables, hazardous activities, and potential public relations problems, present special concerns. Other issues include security, traffic flow and parking, and cooperation with public authorities and law enforcement agencies.

The inclusion of gambling, luxury-item auctions, outdoor venues, and serving alcohol create new risks for the nonprofit. These activities may require special licenses or permits. In addition, the nonprofit's insurance policies may not cover these risks adequately.

RISK MODIFICATION TECHNIQUES FOR HOSTING SPECIAL EVENTS

Screening and training employees and volunteers working at the event are essential to a safe and successful event. Determine in advance who will perform specific tasks, such as handling money, serving alcohol, or providing transportation to minimize mishaps. Special procedures should be put in place for the handling of money or other valuables. If transportation is involved, all drivers should demonstrate that they have a current driver's license, are qualified to drive the vehicles used, and are trained in safety. Also check to see if your state requires any special training for individuals who will be serving alcohol.

One strategy for adequately identifying and managing the risks associated with a special event is to designate a

Risk Management/Safety Committee for the event. The committee should be led by an individual with overall responsibility who is authorized to take action if an emergency arises. The "safety czar" and committee should be involved in all facets of event planning and coordination.

Designate a media spokesperson to handle inquiries about the event. The executive director of a battered women's shelter found herself on the evening news explaining conflicting rumors that had been circulating about the agency's decision to rescind an invitation to an entertainer at an upcoming fund-raiser. Before the event, the entertainer's wife, a wealthy socialite, had died under questionable circumstances. Although the entertainer was not charged in his wife's death, some members of the board decided it was prudent to retract the invitation, and leaked the news to the press. Another board faction invited the entertainer back and leaked *their* decision to the press. Ultimately, the executive director had to explain the board's behavior and the final invitation withdrawal to the media. Any positive impact the event might have had on the shelter's image and visibility was undercut by the poor impression made by the board's actions.

As this example demonstrates, only designated people should talk to the media and everyone associated with the organization — all other employees and volunteers — must know the organization's rules about communications with the media.

RISK SHARING MECHANISMS FOR HOSTING SPECIAL EVENTS

INSURANCE
* *Special events policy.* A commercial general liability policy covers the insured for claims arising out of its opera-

tions. The insurance company calculates the premium based on the nonprofit's operations. Therefore, a homeless shelter is rated on the risks or exposures most commonly expected of such a shelter. The premium charge does not contemplate coverage for a 10K race, dinner dance with auction, or other special fundraising events. In addition, the policy excludes certain activities, such as anything involving automobiles, watercraft, or aircraft. The first step in planning a special event is to check with your nonprofit's insurance advisor to determine if additional insurance coverage is needed. The organization may have to purchase a special events policy.

◆ *Liquor liability coverage.* One unique risk associated with special events is the liability arising from the sale, distribution, serving, or furnishing of alcoholic beverages. The commercial general liability policy usually provides "host liquor liability." "Host liquor" applies to entities not "in the business" of selling, manufacturing, or distributing liquor. Unfortunately, some courts and states have held that an entity *is* in the liquor business if it charges a guest or customer for the drinks (i.e., cash bar or if the admission price includes the furnishing of alcohol). Consequently, a nonprofit may be deemed in the liquor business when selling liquor or when the organization is required to get a liquor license for the event. Check your state's liquor laws and your insurance company's interpretation of "in the business of" to determine if your organization must purchase liquor liability coverage. The coverage is available as either an endorsement to the CGL policy or as a separate policy.

◆ *Coverage for borrowed or leased equipment.* Organizations often borrow or rent equipment for a special event. The property may be tables and chairs, computers, public address systems, or a myriad of other equipment. The commercial general liability policy excludes property damage coverage for personal property within the insured's care, custody, and control. Therefore, the policy will not cover the damage or destruction of borrowed or leased equipment. Check the terms of any rental or lease agreement to determine the organization's contractual requirements. Even if there is no contract, the organization will want to be able to reimburse the property owner for any equipment the organization damaged.

CONTRACTUAL RISK SHARING

One way to transfer or share the risk is to contract with another party, such as a caterer or professional bartenders agency, to provide necessary services. The contract should include an indemnification provision whereby the contractor agrees to pay for specified losses. If the nonprofit transfers financial responsibility to another party, it must obtain documentation that the party accepting the financial responsibility has the resources available to compensate the nonprofit for the losses.

Insurance is a common method for the contractor to fund its indemnification provisions. Request a certificate of insurance from vendors or contractors. An additional technique is to have the nonprofit added as an "additional insured" to the applicable policies.

WAIVERS

Another form of contractual transfer or risk sharing is to use a waiver or release of liability form. Waivers are most commonly used when the special event involves some athletic or recreational activity. The nonprofit requires all participants (or, if they are minors, the legal guardians of participating minors) to sign a waiver before taking part in the activity. When an individual signs a waiver or release of liability, that person surrenders his or her right to sue the organization. The participant accepts the risk of injury and agrees to hold the organization harmless for any injuries resulting from the activity.

For additional information on special event risks, refer to *Managing Special Event Risks: 10 Steps to Safety*, available from the Nonprofit Risk Management Center.

INTERACTING WITH THE PUBLIC
NATURE OF THE RISK

Nonprofit organizations are highly dependent on public support. If the public and donors or funders view the organization negatively, it will be unable to recruit volunteers, employees, and clients and will have difficulty raising funds. The potential loss of goodwill can be devastating to a nonprofit organization. One potential cause of a downturn in public perception is a crisis involving a nonprofit.

A crisis is any sudden situation or event that threatens an organization's ability to fulfill its mission. A crisis may involve death or injury, loss of access to facilities and equipment, disrupted or significantly diminished operations, intense media scrutiny, and possible irreparable damage to a nonprofit's reputation. An agency's response to a crisis can mean the difference between survival and the demise of the organization.

Despite the best risk management program, accidents and crises will occur. A nonprofit's goal is to respond to the situation quickly and to minimize its adverse impact. Crisis planning is key to minimizing the potential loss of goodwill. A crisis plan provides the nonprofit with structure and guidance on how to handle any incident that threat-ens the nonprofit's continued viability. The crisis plan guides the organization's response when the prevention strategies fail or an organization is endangered by a situation beyond its control. The Nonprofit Risk Management Center's publication, *Crisis Management for Nonprofit Organizations: Ten Steps for Survival*, offers a suggested approach to crisis management, including ten steps that can help an agency prepare for and survive a crisis.

RISK MANAGEMENT ISSUES RELATED TO INTERACTING WITH THE PUBLIC

An organization's first goal should be to prevent or avoid any situation that will sour public support or damage its repu-tation. However, when an unfortunate event occurs, the organization must be prepared. The existence of a crisis management plan is crucial to the organization's success in overcoming the adversity. Designating spokesper-sons and developing statements in advance can aid the organization in dealing with the media. Other parts of the plan detail how the organization will respond to the affected parties and resume and restore its operations. The goal of the crisis management plan is for the organization to be prepared to deal effectively with any crisis.

RISK MODIFICATION TECHNIQUES FOR INTERACTING WITH THE PUBLIC

Developing a crisis management plan, including a business resumption plan, is an investment that will pay dividends when a crisis or disaster interrupts the nonprofit's normal business activities. The procedures will help the crisis management team protect and main-tain resources while also protecting, directing, and supporting the agency's employees, volunteers, and clients.

One part of a crisis that is often overlooked is the effect the situation may have on a service partner or funder.

While preparing the plan, review any contractual agreements, especially with a governmental agency or partner in a joint venture. Read the contracts carefully and determine how the nonprofit's ability to deliver services may be affected during a crisis. Plan how the organization will continue to meet its contractual obligations in the event of a crisis.

Establish a communications system and contingency plan for responding to negative publicity. Designate an agency spokesperson (and back-up) to handle media inquiries. Ensure, by means of a briefing and orientation, that employees and volunteers understand their roles in a crisis.

Examine the organization's records to determine if there have been any past crises or disasters. If yes, determine how the organization handled the situation. Identify the lessons learned and incorporate them in the crisis management plan.

RISK SHARING MECHANISMS FOR INTERACTING WITH THE PUBLIC

INSURANCE

No insurance policy covers poor public relations or damage to reputation. At best, insurance can be used as the funding mechanism for compensating the victims of a disaster.

- If the crisis involves the destruction of the nonprofit's facilities, insurance can pay for the direct damage to property.

- In addition, the organization can purchase *business income insurance* to pay for the loss of business income due to an insured event.

- *Extra expense insurance* is important if the organization, such as an emergency shelter or health care provider, must resume operations immediately.

This insurance will pay for the extra expenses incurred to resume operations quickly, including express shipments, higher rent for a temporary location, or payroll for "nonessential" personnel. Discuss the nonprofit's need for business income and extra expense insurance with your insurance advisor.

CONTRACTUAL AGREEMENTS

The potential loss of goodwill cannot be transferred or shared with another. However, under a business resumption plan an organization can establish reciprocal agreements with other organizations or contractors. The organization may be able to negotiate with an organization for access to its computer system, temporary office space, supplemental supplies, or other goods and services. The nonprofit may be able to have another nonprofit provide services to its clients while it is rebuilding after a property loss. Determine which services are critical to your agency's operation and identify ways to ensure that the services will be provided in the event of a loss.

ADMINISTERING EMPLOYMENT POLICIES
NATURE OF THE RISK

Employment-related claims are one of the fastest growing sources of claims for organizations in both the public and private sectors. During fiscal year 1998, nearly 80,000 charges were filed with the Equal Employment Opportunity Commission (EEOC). This number does not include claims filed with state and local regulatory agencies, or lawsuits filed in courts across the country. In the nonprofit sector, employment-related matters represent the largest share of claims filed under Directors' and Officers' (D&O) liability policies.

The Nonprofits' Insurance Alliance of California (NIAC), a charitable risk pool, reports that 87 percent of all claims filed under D&O policies allege wrongful employment actions, ranging from wrongful termination (60%) to sexual harassment (17%) and discrimination (10%). Unfortunately, due to the publicity of multi-million dollar awards and the continued pressure on organizations to do more with less, there is little hope that the trend will reverse.

While most organizations are successful in defending employment claims, the costs — both in financial and human resource terms — of mounting a defense can be significant. Nonprofits must tread carefully to comply with the growing number of employment-related laws and regulations, to ensure the fair treatment of employees, and to minimize the likelihood of a claim. Complicating matters further, many of these issues also apply to an organization's treatment of volunteer staff.

RISK MANAGEMENT ISSUES RELATED TO ADMINISTERING EMPLOYMENT POLICIES

Some key issues related to this risk are described below.

■ *Written procedures on hiring, discipline, and termination* are essential to promote and ensure fairness, equity, and legal compliance. Your nonprofit may also want to consider a policy on nepotism to avoid problems.

■ *Written policies on issues such as sexual harassment and anti-discrimination* enable nonprofits to establish a framework for decisions and a precedent for corrective action. Equal Employment Opportunity Commission (EEOC) regulations state that an employer is responsible for the acts of its agents and supervisory employees with respect to sexual harassment, whether or not the employer authorized, knew, or should have known of the alleged acts. These regulations apply to any employer (for-profit

or nonprofit) with fifteen or more employees. Many states and local governments have their own employment laws that may be more or less stringent than the federal regulations.

■ *Compliance with federal, state and local laws and regulations* is not strictly limited to harassment and discrimination issues. Nonprofit employers must also consider other areas such as wage and hour laws, fair labor standards, employee benefits administration, and reasonable accommodation measures.

■ *Personnel files* contain sensitive and personal information which must be kept confidential. A statement that your organization, or its staff, may make to another — whether written or spoken — can result in liability, and may be challenged in court if an individual believes his or her reputation has been damaged. Disclosure of inaccurate or sensitive records can lead to additional liability. All employment documentation, including performance reviews or disciplinary memos, should be objective, non-judgmental, and always truthful. Information should be accessible to individuals only on a "need to know" basis. Secure employee files and maintain confidentiality. Exercise similar care with volunteer personnel files.

Also remember that these files may be scrutinized for possible discrimination in any future employment actions. To avoid any suggestion of discrimination, maintain information that may disclose that the employee is a member of a protected class — such as proof of United States citizenship required for authorization to work by Federal law or documentation from attorneys or health care providers regarding necessary work accommodations — in a file separate from the employee's personnel file. The employee file should contain the person's employment application, performance evaluations, and any disciplinary memos.

■ *Grievance procedures* are a valuable tool. In the absence of a mechanism for voicing and settling grievances, employees may turn to less desirable means of making their concerns known, including legal challenges, complaints to governmental agencies, and, in some cases, violence. An established policy for reviewing and settling grievances is a means of diffusing potentially troublesome situations.

RISK MODIFICATION TECHNIQUES FOR ADMINISTERING EMPLOYMENT POLICIES

■ ***Develop concise, written policies on employment matters.*** Clear, written policies on employment matters are a nonprofit's first and best defense against employment-related disputes. Carefully written and up-to-date employee policies provide a thorough explanation of the organization's rules, as well as advance warning of procedures that will be invoked under special circumstances. Documents that are especially important include:

✓ *Screening and interviewing policies.* These policies define and explain the process the nonprofit will use to screen and interview applicants. Of particular importance in any screening or selection process is consistency in the treatment of applicants. Provide an interview guide to all supervisors, and train them in the proper way to interview candidates, including interview do's and don'ts.

✓ *Job descriptions.* A detailed job description is the appropriate starting point in a thorough screening process. Every employee will know what is expected of them from the moment they are first considered for a position.

A job description may allay the fears of an applicant or employee about the skills required to perform satisfactorily. Include the essential functions of the position and the educational, experiential, and physical requirements for the position in every job description.

✓ *Employment applications.* The nonprofit's employment application is an invaluable tool that should be used for paid and volunteer staff positions. Applications should include a statement signed by the applicant giving the nonprofit the right to verify any and all information included on the application. In addition, the applicant should give permission for the nonprofit to conduct appropriate background checks. Applications should be carefully reviewed by appropriate personnel, and key information, including past positions held, should be verified. Unfortunately, a significant percentage of job applicants lie about their education and experience. In light of this fact, the application should provide notice to the applicant that any material misrepresentation or omission subsequently discovered by the nonprofit may result in discharge of the employee.

✓ *Employee handbooks.* An effective handbook provides insight into the nonprofit's philosophy regarding the workplace, including its commitment to treat employees fairly and consistently. In addition, a handbook is the appropriate place to outline the specific benefits to which employees are entitled. A handbook tells an employee both what he or she can expect from the employer and what the employer expects from the employee. While most counsel agree that an employee handbook does not materially alter the "employment at will" doctrine, the courts will require employers to live up to the commitments made in such documents.

■ *Follow a carefully documented procedure and exercise special care when handling terminations*. Perceptions regarding a nonprofit's practices may be tied to the degree to which the policies outlined in the handbook and other documents are followed vigorously. It is crucially important to review policies regularly, update them as needed, and follow them closely. As discussed earlier, terminations are the basis for a significant percentage of employment-related claims. As a result, their handling deserves special attention. The following strategies should be followed when handling employee terminations:

✓ *Respect the employee's privacy rights.* Conduct the termination conference in a manner and location that will not exacerbate the employee's embarrassment. In addition, details about the reasons for the termination should be shared with only those who need to know.

✓ *Be honest about the reasons for the termination.* Many wrongful termination claims stem from an employee's assumptions about the reasons he or she was discharged. Never tell an employee that he is being "laid off" when you are in fact terminating the individual for poor performance. Being candid and honest may be the best way to avoid a claim.

✓ *Empower the employee to determine whether or not she will be terminated.* Except in cases of gross misconduct, give employees the time and opportunity to adjust their performance, correct deficiencies, and meet your standards. One way to do this is by imposing a 30-, 60-, or 90-day "probation period" before terminating an employee.

✓ *Require the independent review of all terminations by a senior manager.* A second review of all terminations, including documents prepared prior to the termination, should be required. This review should be conducted by your legal counsel or a senior manager in the organization well-versed in employment matters.

✓ *Strive for consistency in all employment-related actions, including terminations.* Before terminating any staff member, ask whether another similarly situated employee would have received the same treatment.

✓ *Carefully document the reasons for the termination* and the use of any processes or discipline leading up to the termination, including a probation period, warnings, and work-related deficiencies.

✓ *With the exception of terminations for "gross misconduct," err on the side of giving an employee a chance to correct a problem.*

■ *Carefully document all employment-related actions.* Written summaries of conferences with an employee on performance matters should be developed and included in the employee's personnel file. It is appropriate to request that the employee sign such documents to indicate that he or she has seen the summary and agrees that it accurately reflects the meeting's content. Notices of progressive discipline, including probation, should always be in writing and included in the employee's file.

■ *Conduct thorough, candid annual performance reviews.* Annual performance reviews are an invaluable tool. However, these reviews must be candid and honest or they increase rather than minimize the likelihood of an employment-related claim. An employee who receives a "satisfactory" or higher rating who is subsequently fired for poor performance will no doubt assume that impermissible considerations factored into your decision.

■ *Promptly investigate all allegations of harassment or discrimination.* Thorough investigations of allegations are critically important in minimizing the likelihood of a claim. Many plaintiffs in employment cases take their grievances to court when they feel that their concerns or complaints have been ignored.

■ *Seek the advice of counsel before taking action.* The advice of an employment law specialist is invaluable in minimizing the likelihood of a claim. If your current outside counsel (paid or pro bono) does not have experience in this area, it is well worth your time and effort to line someone up who can assist you as matters arise.

■ *Train managers and supervisors in proper personnel techniques.* Many employment-related claims result from the actions of untrained managers and supervisors. The supervisor "shoots from the hip" and takes inappropriate actions against an employee. Ensure that all supervisors know the applicable employment laws, your personnel policies and procedures, and where to go for additional guidance.

One training resource is *Managing Employment Practices*, a four module, interactive, computer-based training program developed by Guided Learning Systems and the Nonprofit Risk Management Center.

Risk Sharing Mechanisms for Employment Practices Liability

Insurance
Employment-related claims have grown substantially in the last few years, as evidenced by a dramatic increase in charges filed with the EEOC. Organizations being sued by employees search for coverage under their insurance policies, often looking first to the commercial general liability policy for coverage — with mixed results. Insurance companies contend it was never the purpose of such policies to provide coverage for employment-related claims, and most companies now attach an employment practices liability exclusion to their CGL policies.

Directors' and Officers' (D&O) Liability policies are also a place organizations seek coverage. After all, neglect on the part of the board, senior managers, and supervisors in properly supervising and monitoring the organization's employment practices is often cited in employment-related claims. However, with the nature of employment claims expanding, many claims may not fit under the traditional definition of a "wrongful act," or be excluded under many D&O policies. Therefore, many insurance companies have developed specific employment practices liability coverage.

Employment practices liability (EPL) coverage is available as either a part of a D&O policy or as a separate policy. There is no standard EPL policy, so coverages vary by insurance company. Policies generally provide defense and indemnity coverage for claims arising out of the employment relationship. An EPL policy may provide coverage for claims alleging discrimination, sexual harassment, wrongful termination, breach of employment contract, failure to employ or promote, wrongful discipline, failure to grant tenure, and negligent evaluation. Since each policy is different, each organization must evaluate its exposures and consult with its insurance advisor to purchase the coverage that best fits its needs.

Collaborating With Others
Nature of the Risk
Although total private giving to charitable organizations rose in 1995, the long-term trend has slowed signifi-

cantly. And while total private giving grew at a marginal rate from 1990 to 1994, corporate giving, measured in constant dollars, fell dramatically over the same period. As a result, it has become increasingly difficult for non-profits to generate revenue to support operations, and the competition for a shrinking pool of charitable dollars has become ever more intense.

Many nonprofit managers and boards believe that in order to survive, they must pursue cooperative, revenue-producing ventures with other organizations. Collaborative undertakings are initiated to find efficiencies or economies of scale in service delivery and to join forces for fund raising. Some non-profits are even joining with corporations in cause-related marketing alliances. A nonprofit must be cautious in approaching collaborative ventures, since its image, visibility, and resources are at stake.

RISK MANAGEMENT ISSUES RELATED TO COLLABORATING WITH OTHERS

The specific details of the partnership are the key to the success or failure of these types of ventures. Community-serving nonprofits need to consider the following issues:

■ *Amount of resources to be devoted to building the collaborative effort.* Every nonprofit should determine how much time, effort, and possible funding will be devoted to establishing the venture.

■ *Potential for reduced donations from traditional donors.* The success of the venture may make current donors think that their support is no longer necessary.

■ *Public reputation of the collaborative partner(s).* The nonprofit's public image could be altered or damaged by association with a corporation or other

organization whose products or practices have come under scrutiny.

■ *Increased reliance on revenue from the collaboration.* If the collaboration becomes a long-term effort, then the nonprofit might become accustomed to receiving a certain portion of its revenue from this source. This increased reliance could have a dampening effect on development and fund-raising activities.

RISK MODIFICATION TECHNIQUES FOR COLLABORATING WITH OTHERS

Clear communication is essential in collaborative ventures. Nonprofits need to be explicit about objectives, measurements of success, the types of resources each party will commit, and the areas for which each will be responsible. The collaboration should have a well-crafted memorandum of understanding or other documentation that specifies the terms of partnership, performance objectives, and accountabilities. If the partnership is with a corporation, an organization must make certain that:

✓ *The corporation does not engage in business practices that conflict with the nonprofit's mission and focus.*

✓ *The partnership enjoys the support of the company's senior managers.* Without a high level commitment, the project may be doomed to failure.

✓ *The firm intends to provide adequate financial support beyond the initial campaign.*

✓ *The corporation will not place undue restrictions on the nonprofit's activities or otherwise interfere with its operations.*

RISK SHARING MECHANISMS FOR COLLABORATING WITH OTHERS

INSURANCE
Both organizations must coordinate their insurance coverages. If the venture

involves cause-related marketing, the nonprofit should be added as an "additional insured" to the corporate partner's commercial general liability (including products coverage) policy. Other insurance requirements will depend upon the nature of the agreement.

CONTRACTUAL TRANSFER

The memorandum of understanding, or contract, is the most important aspect of the collaboration. The details must be specified, written, and acknowledged by both parties. The insurance and indemnification provisions should be reviewed by an insurance professional and legal counsel.

SOLICITING AND MANAGING RESTRICTED FUNDS (GRANTS)
NATURE OF THE RISK

For many nonprofits, an important category of risk emerges when an agency applies for and receives restricted grant funding. As unrestricted funding from foundations and government agencies becomes increasingly rare, restrictive awards are more common. The tremendous competition for grant funds increases the risk that a nonprofit will make promises the organization is unable to keep. Such promises may include overly ambitious goals in terms of client services, or they may relate to meeting administrative "strings" associated with the grant.

The failure by a nonprofit to manage grant funds wisely and live up to its service delivery promises can lead to adverse publicity, litigation, criminal prosecution, and the revocation of grant funding. Nonprofit managers who are tuned in to the risks of accepting restricted funds will first avoid making promises that are difficult or impossible to keep. Then they will take steps to prevent careless mistakes and establish controls to detect and correct problems quickly. The successful management of restricted grant funds is possible when managers:

■ *Carefully weigh the costs and benefits* associated with each grant-funding opportunity and apply cautiously for funding.

■ *Take the time required to fully understand donor requirements and expectations.*

■ *Plan ahead, organize effectively, and communicate with staff* to ensure that requirements and expectations are understood and met.

■ *Take immediate action when problems occur.*

RISK MANAGEMENT ISSUES RELATED TO SOLICITING AND MANAGING RESTRICTED FUNDS

Whether your nonprofit promises too much in the final throes of negotiating a grant or takes on a project you are ill-equipped to handle alone, many different things can go wrong in the solicitation and management of grant funds. Complicated "strings" are increasingly common in the current era of private philanthropy and government grant making.

It is also difficult to ensure that total spending on a restricted program does not exceed grant revenues. Even when indirect costs are allowed, there are frequently uncovered expenses. In many instances, grants cost nonprofits more than they bring in. In addition, restricted grants encourage institutional growth and/or special projects that may not be sustainable in the long term. A nonprofit can easily fall into the trap of hiring project staff and failing to let them go after a funding cycle concludes.

RISK MODIFICATION TECHNIQUES FOR SOLICITING AND MANAGING RESTRICTED FUNDS

■ *Pursue restricted grants with caution and accept the temporary nature of all projects supported with restricted funds.*

■ *Acknowledge, identify, and monitor the strings which accompany a restricted grant.* Begin by carefully reading all grant agreements, donor letters, and other funding documents. Make certain you are clear about what you will do, where you will do it, and when each task is to be completed. Before work begins, compare the proposal with the actual funding agreement for consistency. Periodically during the funding period, reread the grant conditions and scope of work and determine whether you are in compliance. If changes are necessary and key deliverables are no longer feasible, discuss the matter with your funder and document changes in writing.

■ *Carefully monitor expenditures for restricted grant projects to ensure that total spending does not exceed grant revenues.* Also institute controls to ensure that a grantor's funds will be used only to support projects specified in, or appropriate under, the grant. When grant revenues exceed expenditures, seek written permission to reallocate the money to another budget item within the grant. Otherwise, excess revenues must be returned to the grantor.

■ *Avoid restricted grants that require institutional growth or projects that may not be sustainable once the funding cycle is over.*

■ *Plan carefully and communicate expectations to key parties.* Outline responsibilities and authority levels for each staff person assigned to the grant. In most instances, the designation of a "project manager" for each grant is appropriate. That individual should be held responsible for service delivery as well as administrative matters concerning the grant. Encourage staff to document information related to grant deliverables and establish a system for filing information on grant-funded projects so that it is readily accessible.

■ *Always assess your grant-seeking practices, prospective funders, and partnership opportunities in relation to the organization's mission and goals.* Will receiving a grant further enable the nonprofit to fulfill its mission and maintain its public trust? Does the nonprofit's request for assistance make sense in terms of the grant-making agency's mission?

RISK SHARING MECHANISMS FOR SOLICITING AND MANAGING RESTRICTED FUNDS

INSURANCE
No insurance policy covers all of the potential consequences of failing to meet a funder's expectations. These consequences include the need to return funds, the loss of future funding, and negative publicity. A directors' and officers' (D&O) liability policy should, however, provide funds for, or reimburse the organization for defense costs and any final award in a third-party (funder) claim alleging mismanagement of grant funds.

Proper financial safeguards should be in place to prevent an employee from stealing funds or other resources from the program. In addition, an Employee Dishonesty policy offers protection should an employee embezzle or steal the funds associated with the grant.

CONTRACTUAL TRANSFER
Many grants involve partnership arrangements which may be necessary to fulfill grant obligations. For example, a nonprofit may use independent contractors to support service delivery

funded under a restricted grant, such as a commercial transportation provider, market research firm or other organization. Losses stemming from the mismanagement of a grant, however, cannot be transferred completely to another organization unless that organization is a party to the underlying agreement. Unless the grant agreement contains mutually binding agreements with these contractors, their performance (or failure to perform) is ultimately the responsibility of the nonprofit.

A nonprofit should attempt to transfer the risks controlled by the contractor or service provider to that contractor. In most cases, however, the true risks associated with the contractor's performance are retained by the nonprofit. Managing restricted grants wisely requires the careful evaluation of contractor capabilities and the close monitoring of performance. Determine which outside services are necessary to fulfill the grant obligations and identify ways to ensure that the services will be provided in a timely fashion. Also, make certain that the nonprofit will be compensated if the contractor fails to perform. Once you have identified the service provider, negotiate a hold harmless agreement and indemnification provisions from the contractor for damages resulting from their negligence. These agreements should be supported by adequate financing. In most cases, this means that the contractor should have appropriate insurance coverages and limits, adding the nonprofit as an additional insured to the contractor's policy.

SUMMARY

Community-serving nonprofits face an array of unique or special risks. These risks can be addressed — but only once they are identified and analyzed. The risk management techniques most frequently employed are those that modify the risks to make them acceptable to the organization. However, sometimes the avoidance option must be used if the activity is too risky and uncontrollable.

Purchasing insurance is a common risk sharing technique. While insurance is available for many risks, the affordability of insurance is an issue for the vast majority of the nation's nonprofit organizations. Also, insurance is just one small part of an effective risk management program. Contracts, indemnification provisions, and waivers are also effective risk sharing techniques. Every nonprofit should secure legal counsel and an insurance professional's review of any contracts or waivers.

Special risks require special action. An organization's attention to risk management may be the difference between a successful program and an unfortunate accident that threatens the survival of the nonprofit.

CHAPTER 5

Glossary of Terms

This glossary is designed to be a reference for nonprofit managers and volunteers responsible for risk management. The definitions are applicable to the nonprofit sector. Although accurate, the definitions vary from those the reader might find in a law dictionary or insurance text.

Accident
Unexpected or chance event. This term is frequently defined in older commercial general liability (CGL) policies.

Actual cash value (ACV)
Replacement cost of damaged or lost property less depreciation.

Actual damages
(also known as compensatory damages) Sum of money a plaintiff (injured party) is entitled to, to compensate him for actual economic loss sustained.

Auto insurance
Business Auto Policy (BAP) - A standard business automobile policy that is designed to cover the liability and physical damage of motor vehicles. Liability coverage can be provided for the organization, regardless of whether a nonprofit, a staff member, volunteer or other party owns the vehicle.

Avoidance
Risk management strategy in which a nonprofit avoids an activity or service that it considers too risky.

Board of directors
Governance body of a nonprofit made up of individuals who are appointed or elected and whose function it is to provide policy, and sometimes management, and direction for the purpose of accomplishing the organization's mission.

Boiler and Machinery/ Equipment insurance
Insurance coverage that protects against damage caused by the sudden and accidental breakdown of mechanical, electrical or refrigeration systems. This coverage pays for the property damage, any consequential damage (such as spoiled food from the breakdown of a refrigerator) and any amount for which the nonprofit is liable, subject to policy limits.

Business income insurance (business interruption insurance)

Insurance coverage designed to protect the insured against loss of earnings resulting from the interruption of business caused by an insured peril, subject to the policy provisions.

Bylaws

Set of rules that outline how a nonprofit organization operates, including rules describing key positions and their respective duties, election of officers, frequency of board meetings, and quorum requirements.

Care, Duty of

Standard of behavior required by a nonprofit board member or officer in making decisions. The standard is to use the level of care that a reasonably prudent person would exercise in a similar situation.

Casualty insurance

A category of insurance that offers protection against claims resulting from negligent acts, errors, or omissions that cause bodily injury or property damage to others. Commonly referred to as liability insurance.

Certificate of insurance

A form that indicates the types of insurance policies written, policy dates, and coverage limits.

Charitable immunity

Legal defense, now largely defunct, by which charitable organizations were protected from litigation by virtue of their charitable status.

Commercial General Liability (CGL) insurance

Insurance that covers claims filed by another party (i.e. clients, general public) alleging bodily injury, personal injury and/or property damage arising from the nonprofit's premises or operations.

Deductible

Amount deducted from a loss. The deductible is an amount assumed in advance by an insured as a means of obtaining a lower premium for the coverage.

Defendant

Individual or organization against whom a lawsuit has been brought.

Directors' & Officers' (D&O) liability insurance

Insurance that provides coverage against "wrongful acts" which might include actual or alleged errors, omissions, misleading statements, and neglect or breach of duty on the part of the board of directors and other insured persons and entities.

Employee

Individual who is paid to perform specific duties under the direction and control of the organization. The individual is provided with a wage or salary, and sometimes benefits.

Employment Practices Liability Insurance (EPLI)

Insurance that provides coverage for claims arising out of employment practices. EPLI policies generally cover the organization, its directors, officers, and employees.

Endorsement

Document specifying changes to the coverage afforded by a specific insurance policy.

Excess Automobile Liability insurance

Auto liability insurance that covers claims arising from a volunteer's or employee's use of their own vehicle. This policy pays on behalf of the volunteer or employee in excess of the individual's personal auto policy. No coverage is provided to the nonprofit.

Exclusion
Provision within an insurance policy that specifies the perils or conditions that are not covered.

Fidelity bond
A bond that reimburses an employer, up to the stated amount, in the event that an employee commits a dishonest act covered by the bond. Also known as Employee Dishonesty coverage.

Fund raising
The process by which a nonprofit organization solicits and obtains donations (monetary, in-kind, or other categories) for general or specified purposes in order to achieve its mission.

Goodwill
An organization's reputation, stature in the community, and the ability to raise funds and appeal to prospective volunteers.

Grant
The transfer of money or property from one entity, usually a charitable foundation or governmental entity, to another (either an individual or charitable organization), to enable the recipient to offer some service or charitable benefit.

Hazard
A condition that may create or increase the possibility of a loss due to a peril.

Hold harmless agreement
Contract by which legal liability for damages of one party is assumed by the other party.

Immunity
A provision in the law which shields a person or organization from legal obligations.

Income
An organization's revenue, i.e. sales, grants, investment earnings and contributions.

Indemnify
Compensate for actual losses sustained.

Informed Consent
The assumption of liability by a volunteer or service recipient following the identification of specific hazards by a sponsor organization.

Insurance
A contract whereby an organization agrees to indemnify another and/or to pay a specified amount for covered losses in exchange for a premium.

Joint and several liability
A form of liability in which all of the individuals involved are fully liable as individuals and also as members of a group.

Joint liability
A form of liability in which liability is shared by more than one person or organization.

Joint venture
A business endeavor in which two or more parties combine their resources for a single undertaking and share profits and losses as agreed upon. A joint venture is usually unincorporated and limited in scope and duration. A commercial general liability policy generally does not cover a joint venture unless it is listed as an insured.

Liability
Any enforceable legal obligation. For example, the failure to meet the duty of care of a reasonable person under similar circumstances.

Litigation
Describes the activities that emerge from a lawsuit or legal proceeding. The nonprofit receives a summons, and must defend itself in court.

Loyalty, Duty of
Standard of behavior that requires a director or officer (of a board) to pursue the interests of the organization, particularly financial, rather than his/her own or the interests of another person.

To place the organization's interests ahead of his/her own.

Mailing list
List of names and addresses of individuals. Nonprofits often compile mailing lists as a fundraising tool, or as a means of sending information to individiuals who have expressed interest in the organization.

Minutes
Minutes are a summary of a board meeting. The specifications for acceptable minutes will vary with the organization, but should include who attended the meeting, the significant issues discussed, the actions taken on motions and resolutions, and reports of officers or committees.

Modification
Modification is a risk management technique and means of changing the activity so that the chance of harm occurring and impact of potential damage are within acceptable limits.

Negligence
Failure to use the standard of care that a reasonably prudent person would exercise in a similar circumstance.

Nonowned auto insurance
Insurance protection for the organization against liability arising from the use of a vehicle not owned by the nonprofit, but by someone acting on behalf of the organization, such as an employee, volunteer or independent contractor.

Nonprofit Corporation Act
State legislation that provides for the establishment and operation of nonprofit corporations. The legislation outlines the rights and duties of nonprofit corporations in addition to specifying rules for the election of officers, holding of meetings and procedures for the dissolution, liquidation, or other changes in the organization's legal status.

Nonprofit (or not-for-profit) organization
An organization in which no part of its income is distributable to its members, directors, officers, stockholders or other individuals and that meets the state statute designation of a nonprofit entity. *Note:* while most people equate nonprofit organizations with charitable or 501(c)(3) entities (those that are eligible to receive tax deductible contributions), other categories of nonprofits exist as well, including trade associations and labor unions. An organization need not be tax-exempt to be recognized and organized as a "nonprofit" under state law.

Nonprofit sector
(also called independent sector, charitable sector, voluntary sector or tax-exempt sector) – A collection of organizations that are formally constituted, private (as opposed to governmental), serve some public purpose, self-governing, voluntary, and non-profit-distributing.

Obedience, Duty of
Standard of care that obligates a director or officer (of a board) to act in a manner that demonstrates faithfulness to the organization's mission and obeys all applicable laws, statutes and regulations.

Occupational accident
Accident to an employee that occurs within and arises out of the course of employment.

Officer
Individual who has a fiduciary responsibility within a nonprofit. This individual can be a member of the organization's board, executive committee, or an employee of the organization.

People
Category of nonprofit assets at risk that includes board members, volunteers, employees, clients, donors, and the general public.

Personal injury liability
Injury to a person or organization caused by slander, invasion of privacy, false arrest or detention, malicious prosecution, or wrongful entry or eviction.

Personally liable
Liability that an individual assumes when he/she is directly involved in the occurrence and cannot defer the liability to another person or entity.

Plaintiff
Individual or organization that initiates a lawsuit to obtain a remedy for an injury.

Property
Category of nonprofit assets at risk that includes real property (buildings, improvements and betterments), personal property (furniture, fixtures, valuable papers and records, equipment, and supplies) and intangible property (copyrights, business goodwill and trademarks).

Property insurance
Insurance that covers direct damage to the nonprofit's property including consequential losses (business income, loss of rents, extra expense) caused by an insured peril.

Prudent person rule
Legal rule that individuals are expected to act with the same degree of care that a reasonably prudent individual would demonstrate in a similar situation.

Punitive damages
Damages awarded by the court to an individual in excess of those required to compensate the plaintiff for the loss sustained. These damages are a type of punishment for the offender for failing to take proper care.

Quorum
The minimum number of individuals required in the bylaws to be present to conduct business at a meeting.

Respondeat superior
Legal principle by which employers are held responsible for the actions of those they supervise. Literally, the "master" shall answer for the acts of his "servant." In the context of volunteer organizations, the nonprofit is the "master" and paid and volunteer staff are the "servants" working on the organization's behalf.

Retention
A tool or technique in risk management whereby the nonprofit accepts all or a portion of the risk and prepares for the consequences. A deductible on an insurance policy is a form of retention.

Risk
Any threat or possibility of loss that will endanger an organization's ability to accomplish its mission.

Risk evaluation and prioritization
A step in the risk management process that examines the possibility of each risk becoming reality and estimates its probable effect and cost to the nonprofit.

Risk identification
The first step in the risk management process that identifies the risks that are relevant to the organization.

Risk management
A discipline for dealing with the possibility that a future event will cause harm.

Risk management techniques
Strategies for controlling risk which include avoidance, modification, retention, and sharing.

Risk management process

A four-step process nonprofits undertake to control risk: (1) acknowledge and identify risk, (2) evaluate and prioritize risk, (3) select and implement risk management techniques, and (4) monitor and update the risk management plan.

Risk modification

Changing an activity so that the chance of harm occurring and affect of potential damage are within acceptable limits.

Risk sharing

A risk management tool whereby an organization shares risk with another organization. Examples of risk sharing include mutual aid agreements with other nonprofits, purchasing insurance, and sharing responsibility for a risk with another through a contractual agreement.

Staff

Paid and volunteer personnel who carry out the work of an organization.

Vicarious liability

Liability imposed on a person or organization for the acts, errors or omissions of persons serving on its behalf.

Vicarious liability can be imposed even if the individual or organization is not directly involved in the occurrence. The liability of one party is imputed to another.

Volunteer

Individual who freely provides services to an organization without compensation other than reimbursement for reasonable expenses.

Waiver

The giving up of a right or privilege. Nonprofits frequently require participants in recreational or other programs to waive the right to sue in the event of injury. Courts often invalidate waivers on the grounds that the individual did not fully appreciate the rights being waived or that the waiver did not specifically indicate that it covered liability for negligence.

Workers compensation

Insurance that insures the employer's responsibilities for injuries, disability or death to persons in his/her employ, as prescribed by law.

Sources

Giftis, Steven H. *Law Dictionary.* Woodbury, N.Y.: Barron's Educational Series, Inc., 1975.

Hopkins, Bruce R. *Nonprofit Law Dictionary.* New York: John Wiley & Sons, Inc., 1994.

Lai, Mary L., Terry S. Chapman, and Elmer L. Steinbock. *Am I Covered For...?* 2d ed., San Jose, CA: Human Services Inc., 1984.

Lorimer, James J., Harry P. Perlet, Rederick G. Kempkin, and Frederick H. Hodosh. *The Legal Environment of Insurance, Volumes I and II.* Malvern, PA: AICPCU

Salamon, Lester M. *America's Nonprofit Sector: A Primer*, The Foundation Center, 1992.

CHAPTER 6

Resource Organizations and Bibliography

AMERICAN SOCIETY FOR HEALTHCARE RISK MANAGEMENT
1 N. Franklin Street
Chicago, IL 60606
(312) 422-3980

INDEPENDENT SECTOR
1828 L Street, NW
Washington, DC 20036
Telephone: (202) 223-8100
website: www.indepsec.org

Independent Sector provides information, advocacy and services for philanthropy, charities and volunteerism. The organization strives to enhance the capacity for the nonprofit sector to achieve excellence.

INTERNATIONAL RISK MANAGEMENT INSTITUTE, INC. (IRMI)
12222 Merit Drive, # 1450
Dallas, TX 75251-2276
Telephone: (800) 827-4242
(972) 960-7693 (Dallas)
website: www.irmi.com

IRMI is a publisher of risk management and insurance reference manuals, books,

and newsletters. The publications give practical information to interpret insurance policies and arrange a comprehensive risk management program.

NATIONAL CENTER FOR NONPROFIT BOARDS
Suite 510-W
2000 L Street, NW
Washington, DC 20036-4907
Telephone: (800) 883-6262
website: www.ncnb.org

National Center for Nonprofits Boards is dedicated to improving the effectiveness of nonprofit organizations by strengthening boards. The Center offers publications, education, and consulting services to nonprofit organizations.

NATIONAL COUNCIL OF NONPROFIT ASSOCIATIONS (NCNA)
1900 L Street, NW, Suite 605
Washington, DC 20036-5024
Telephone: (202) 467-6262
FAX: (202) 467-6261
website: www.ncna.org

The National Council of Nonprofit Associations is a national network of state-based associations that collectively represents more than 20,000 community nonprofits. The NCNA network responds to the diverse needs of community nonprofits, offering management support and technical assistance, advocacy and public education, cost-saving products and services, and professional development opportunities. Visit NCNA's website (www.ncna.org) for information on the association in your state.

NONPROFIT RISK MANAGEMENT CENTER
1001 Connecticut Avenue, NW
Suite 410
Washington, DC 20036
Telephone: (202) 785-3891
FAX: (202) 296-0349
website: www.nonprofitrisk.org

The Nonprofit Risk Management Center is dedicated to helping community-serving nonprofits control risk. The Center offers informative workshops and seminars, publishes books, resource guides and pamphlets, and offers consulting services and technical assistance on a wide range of risk management, liability and insurance issues.

POINTS OF LIGHT FOUNDATION
1737 H Street, NW
Washington, DC 20006
Telephone: (202) 223- 9186

The *Volunteer Community Service Catalogue* offers a large collection of publications, videos, and other tools for volunteer programs. Call or write for your free copy.

PUBLIC RISK MANAGEMENT ASSOCIATION (PRIMA)
1815 N. Fort Myer Drive, Suite 1020
Arlington, VA 22209
Telephone: (703) 528-7701
website: www.primacentral.org

PRIMA promotes and encourages effective risk management in public agencies and promotes and advances the profession of risk management as an integral part of public administration. PRIMA offers education and training, publications, professional development, research and a valuable resource for all organizations.

RISK AND INSURANCE MANAGEMENT SOCIETY (RIMS)
655 Third Avenue
New York, NY 10007
Telephone: (202) 286-9292
website: www.rims.org

RIMS is a professional organization dedicated to advancing the practice of risk management. RIMS is the world's largest association for risk management representing all sectors and serves individual risk managers through 96 chapters across the United States and Canada.

SOCIETY FOR NONPROFIT ORGANIZATIONS
6314 Odana Road, Suite 1
Madison, WI 53719
Telephone: (800) 424-7367
web site: http://danenet.wicip.org/snpo/

The Society provides training and publications about nonprofit operations and management. Call or write for a free catalogue.

Bibliography and Selected Resources

Andreasen, Alan R. "Profits for Nonprofits: Find a Corporate Partner." *Harvard Business Review*. November/December, 1996.

Bachman, Steve. *Nonprofit Litigation: A Practical Guide with Forms and Checklists.* New York: John Wiley & Sons, Inc. 1994.

Bernstein, Peter L. *Against the Gods: The Remarkable Story of Risk.* New York: John Wiley & Sons, Inc. 1996.

Bryson, John M. *Strategic Planning for Public and Nonprofit Organizations.* San Francisco: Jossey-Bass Publishers, 1988.

Burton, K. *The Non-Lawyers Non-Profit Corporation Kit.* Tucson, AZ: Alpha Publications of America, 1992.

Carver, John. *Boards That Make a Difference.* San Francisco: Jossey-Bass, 1990.

Connors, Tracy Daniel (Ed. in Chief). *The Nonprofit Handbook.* 2d ed. New York: McGraw-Hill Book Company, 1988.

Connors, Tracy Daniel. *The Volunteer Management Handbook.* New York: John Wiley & Sons, Inc., 1994.

Drucker, Peter F. *Managing the Non-Profit Organization.* New York: Harper Collins, 1990.

Drucker, Peter F. *How to Assess Your Nonprofit Organization with Peter Drucker's Five Most Important Questions: A User's Guide for Boards, Staff, Volunteers.* San Francisco: Jossey-Bass Publishers, 1992.

Duca, Diane J. *Nonprofit Boards: Roles, Responsibilities and Performance.* New York: John Wiley & Sons, Inc., 1996.

Fisher, J. C. and K. M. Cole. *Leadership and Management of Volunteer Programs.* San Francisco: Jossey-Bass Publishers, 1993.

Greenfeld, James M. *Fund Raising Cost Effectiveness: A Self Assessment Workbook.* New York: John Wiley & Sons, Inc. 1994.

Greenfeld, James M. *Fund Raising: Evaluating and Managing the Fund Development Process.* New York: John Wiley & Sons, Inc., 1995.

Hadden, Elaine M. and Balire A. French. *Nonprofit Organizations: Rights and Liabilities for Members, Directors, and Officers.* Wilmette, IL.: Callaghan, 1987.

Herman, Melanie L. and Leslie T. White. *Leaving Nothing to Chance: Achieving Board Accountability Through Risk Management,* Washington, DC: National Center for Nonprofit Boards and Nonprofit Risk Mangement Center, 1998.

Herman, Melanie L. and Leslie T. White. *D&O: What You Need to Know,* Washington, DC: Nonprofit Risk Mangement Center, 1998.

Herman, Robert D. *Executive Leadership in Nonprofit Organizations: New Strategies for Shaping Executive-Board Dynamics.* San Francisco: Jossey-Bass, 1991.

Hopkins, Bruce R. *Charity, Advocacy, and the Law.* New York: John Wiley & Sons, Inc., 1994.

Hopkins, Bruce R. *The Law of Fundraising.* 2d ed. New York: John Wiley & Sons, Inc., 1994.

Hopkins, Bruce R. *A Legal Guide to Starting and Managing a Nonprofit Organization.* 2d ed. New York: John Wiley & Sons, Inc., 1993.

Knauft, E.B., Renee A. Berger, and Sandra T. Gray. *Profiles of Excellence.* San Francisco: Jossey-Bass, 1991.

Kritt, Robert L. *The Fundraising Handbook.* Dubuque, IA: Kendall/Hunt Publishing Co., 1993.

Landskroner, Ronald A. *The Nonprofit Manager's Resource Directory.* New York: John Wiley & Sons, Inc., 1993.

Leifer, Jacqueline C. and Michael B. Glomb. *The Legal Obligations of Nonprofit Boards.* Washington, DC: National Center for Nonprofit Boards, 1993.

Masaoka, Jan.   *Action Handbook for Boards*. San Francisco: Support Center for Nonprofit Management, 1995.

McIntyre, William S., Jack P. Gibson, and Robert A. Bregman. *101 Ways to Cut Business Insurance Costs Without Sacrificing Protection*. Dallas, TX: International Risk Management Institutes, Inc., 1995.

Minnesota Office on Volunteer Services. *Planning It Safe: How to Control Liability and Risk in Volunteer Programs*. St. Paul, MN, 1992.

Oleck, Howard L. and Martha E. Stewart. *Nonprofit Corporations, Organizations and Associations*. 6th ed, Englewood Cliffs, NJ: Prentice Hall, 1994.

Oleck, Howard L. and C. Green. *Parliamentary Law and Practice for Nonprofit Organizations*. Philadelphia: American Law Institute, American Bar Association, 1991.

Overton, G. W. (Ed.). *Guidebook for Directors of Nonprofit Corporations*. Chicago, IL: American Bar Association, 1993.

Patterson, John and Pamela Rypkema. *Crisis Management for Nonprofit Organizations: Ten Steps for Survival*. Washington, DC: Nonprofit Risk Management Center, 1996.

Patterson, John. *Staff Screening Tool Kit: Building a Strong Foundation Through Careful Staffing*. Washington, DC: Nonprofit Risk Management Center, 1998.

Robinson, Maureen K. *Developing the Nonprofit Board*. Washington, DC: National Center for Nonprofit Boards, 1994.

Salamon, L.   *America's Nonprofit Sector: A Primer*. Baltimore, MD: The Johns Hopkins University, 1991.

Scheff, Joanne and Philip Kotler. "How the Arts Can Prosper Through Strategic Collaborations." *Harvard Business Review*, January/February 1996.

Seidman, Anna, and John Patterson. *Kidding Around? Be Serious! A Commitment to Safe Service Opportunities for Your People.* Washington, DC: Nonprofit Risk Management Center, 1996.

Singer, Barbara. *Nonprofit Organizations: Operations Handbook for Directors and Administrators.* Wilmette, IL.: Callaghan & Co., 1987.

Smith, Barry D., and Eric A. Wiening. *How Insurance Works.* Malvern, Insurance Institutes of America, 1994.

Smith, Bucklin & Associates. *The Complete Guide to Nonprofit Management.* New York: John Wiley & Sons, Inc., 1996.

Tremper, Charles R., and Gwynne Kostin. *No Surprises: Controlling Risks in Volunteer Programs.* Washington, DC: Nonprofit Risk Management Center, 1993.

Ward, S. L. *Tort Liability of Nonprofit Governing Boards.* New York: Garland Publishing, 1993.

Weisgrau, Toni. "Reference Checks Reduce Hiring Mistakes." *Third Sector Report,* March, 1994.

Notes

Notes